Galaxy Angel
PARTY
D0926003

by Kanan and others

Original Concept by BROCCOLI

Galaxy Angel Party Volume 1

English Adaptation Staff
Translation: Koji Tajii, Satsuki Yamashita
English Adaptation: Jason R. Grissom
Clean-Up, Touch-Up & Lettering: Alex Ahad
Cover & Layout: Chris McDougall

Editor: Satsuki Yamashita, Dietrich Seto
Sales Manager: Ardith D. Santiago
Managing Editor: Shizuki Yamashita
Publisher: Kaname Tezuka, Hideki Uchino

Email: editor@broccolibooks.com
Website: www.bro-usa.com

A BROCCOLI BOOKS Manga
Broccoli Books is a division of Broccoli International USA, Inc.
P.O. Box 66078 Los Angeles CA 90066

First published in Japan in 2003 by BROCCOLI Co., Ltd

ISBN-13: 978-1-9324-8026-9
ISBN-10: 1-932480-26-9

Published by Broccoli International USA, Inc.
First printing, June 2005

www.bro-usa.com

10 9 8 7 6 5 4 3 2 1
Printed in the United States

Table of Contents 

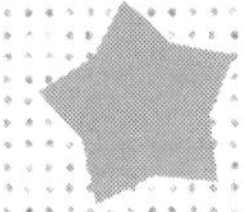

Table of Contents

Milfeulle Sakuraba

****

Milfeulle Sakuraba

Age: 17
Rank: Second Lieutenant
Height: 5'1"

Favorite food: Ice cream, crepes, anything sweet
Hobbies: Cooking (especially snacks), housework in general
Special abilities: Extraordinary luck. She brings both good and bad fortune to those around her.

CONCEPT SKETCHES

Lucky Star

Lucky Star is a well equipped Emblem Frame with various weapons, but the stability of the ship is inconsistent. Only Milfeulle, who has extraordinary luck, can control it.

Milfeulle is a cheerful and easy-going girl. She has a carefree and unmotivated attitude toward her assignments, but can be stubborn about anything she disagrees with. She has extraordinarily good luck, and tries to use it for a good cause.

Ranpha Franboise

****

Ranpha Franboise

Age: 18
Rank: Second Lieutenant
Height: 5'3"

Favorite food: Anything spicy
Hobbies: Fortune-telling
Special abilities: Martial arts

CONCEPT SKETCHES

Kung Fu Fighter

Kung Fu Fighter is Ranpha's Emblem Frame, customized for short-range combat. It is equipped with an electromagnetic wire anchor on both sides of the fighter. It is designed to be light and fast, and its offensive power is very strong. To gain this offensive strength, its defense had to be compromised.

Ranpha is very strong willed. She sees things in terms of black and white, or profit and loss. She can appear pushy at times, but she is also very warmhearted and sentimental (although she would deny it). She may seem arrogant, but she is desperately searching for true love and resorts to fortune telling and charms to find it. She has been Milfeulle's friend since the Academy. Unfortunately for her, however, she always seems to bear the burden of Milfeulle's misadventures. She is well trained in kung fu and rapid hand-to-hand combat. She loves extremely spicy foods.

Ranpha Franboise Profile

Mint Blancmanche

****

Mint Blancmanche

Age: 16
Rank: Second Lieutenant
Height: 4'1"

Favorite food: Junk food with lots of artificial flavoring and color
Hobbies: Cosplay (although she keeps it a secret)
Special abilities: Reading minds

CONCEPT SKETCHES

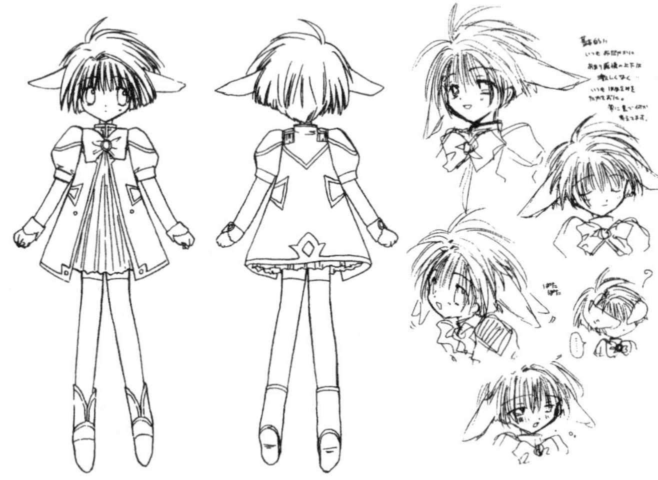

Trick Master

This Emblem Frame is outfitted with a remote-controlled pod-unit called "Flier," suited for long-range attacks. It possesses powerful radar for widespread reconnaissance and is very effective at information analysis. Trick Master is often used as a mobile command center.

Mint seems to be smiling all the time, but she is really a shrewd and slick character who doesn't back down on important matters. She is the only daughter of the Blancmanche Conglomerate, one of the wealthiest families of the galaxy. Due to her strict education, she is adept at strategy and information analysis. It can be said that she is the "brain" of the Angel Troupe. In addition, she has the extraordinary gift of telepathy, which she can use to read people's inner thoughts. This gift has its downside, however, and has caused her to become somewhat distrustful. Mint enjoys artificially flavored and colored junk food, character cosplay and other costumes, and bizarre fashions.

Mint Blancmanche Profile

Forte Stollen

****

Forte Stollen

Age: 22
Rank: First Lieutenant
Height: 5'9"

Favorite food: Yakitori, Oden, anything that goes with alcohol
Hobbies: Guns, missiles
Special abilities: Handling firearms

CONCEPT SKETCHES

Happy Trigger

Happy Trigger is equipped with a wide variety of weapons, including beams, lasers, electromagnetic particles, ion particles and tons of missiles. It boasts the most firepower and the heaviest armor of the five Emblem Frames, which costs it some mobility.

Being the oldest member of the Angel Troupe, Forte is the unofficial "troupe captain." She is known for her frankness and open mindedness. Forte does not let emotion interfere with her work and is overly meticulous about her professional life. She is a gun maniac who sees more beauty in "old-fashioned projectile firearms with a bang" than in modern laser guns. Her shooting skills are of world-class caliber. She likes "old people" foods such as oden and yakitori. Subconsciously, she seems to be slightly sadistic, but the men can't resist her glamorous appearance and ample proportions.

Forte Stollen Profile

Vanilla H

****

Vanilla H

Age: 13
Rank: Second Lieutenant
Height: 4'4"

Favorite food: None in particular (She is a religion-based vegetarian.)
Hobbies: Worshipping, scripture recitation
Special abilities: Healing with her nanotech pet

CONCEPT SKETCHES

Harvester

Harvester can transport a high number of nanomachines for the repair of damaged fighters. It plays a supporting role among the Emblem Frames. Its artillery is weak, but it possesses the strongest defensive system out of the Emblem Frames.

Vanilla is a taciturn girl who does not express her feelings. Although she will answer questions, she rarely speaks on her own. She has a special ability to control nanotechnology and can frequently be seen with a squirrel-like nanotech pet, which is made of a group of microscopic machines. This device enables her to fix any machine and heal any living organism.

Vanilla does everything she is told. She has no personal desires or will, but has a strong sense of duty, which is supported by an almighty faith in her religion.

Normad

****

Normad

Age: Unknown
Rank: Plushie
Height: 1'4"
Special abilities: Extensive knowledge of everything

A character from the Galaxy Angel anime, Normad was once the A.I. of a missile guidance system, boasting a CPU of 10,000 GHz. Now, he inhabits the body of a rather unappealing stuffed animal. His real name is unpronounceably long. He worships and adores Vanilla, but his wisecracks don't win him any friends among the Angels.

Takuto Meyers

****

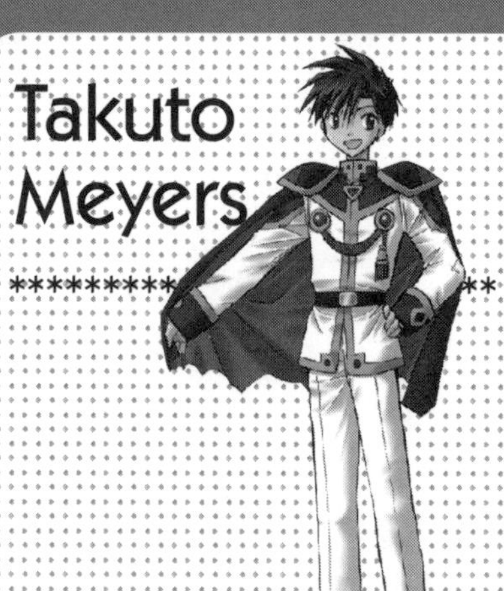

Takuto Meyers

Age: 21
Rank: Captain
Height: 5'5"
Hobbies: Chess, board games in general

Takuto is the carefree commander of the Angel Troupe in the Galaxy Angel videogames and manga. He is an odd soldier, since he dislikes battles, authority, and power. But he is easygoing and can brush off almost anything with a smile. At first glance he seems unremarkable, though on closer inspection, he has a charisma that leads his crew to form a special bond with him. Being a normal guy, he loves cute girls.

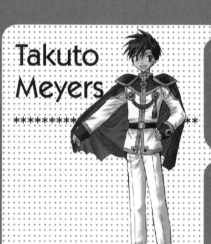

Volcott O. Huey

****

Volcott O. Huey
Age: 55
Rank: Lieutenant Colonel
Height: 6'1"
Hobbies: Chess

Volcott is the middle-aged commander of the Angel Brigade in the anime, and is rumored to have been very sharp witted when he was young. By appearances he stands aloof from the rest of the world, but he is actually very much concerned for the Angel Troupe. Supposedly he was once known as the "White Wolf of the New Galaxy," but no one knows for sure. He's very proud of his neat mustache.

Major Mary

****

Major Mary
Age: Unknown
Rank: Major

Mary is the Perot brothers' superior officer in the anime, and is the creator of Team Twin Star. Once called the "Roaring Golden Meteor," she was both highly admired and feared. She sees Volcott and the Angel Troupe as rivals to Team Twin Star.

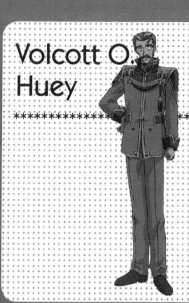

Kokomo Perot

****

Kokomo Perot

Age: 10

Special abilities: Weapons master

Kokomo is hyper and absolutely fearless, but is also simple-minded and naively honest. As such, he's easily coaxed into doing things. Despite his age, he has a high proficiency in the use of various weapons, particularly those involving shooting. Although the younger of the two brothers, he is the leader of Team Twin Star, and he hates to be treated like a kid.

Malibu Perot

****

Malibu Perot

Age: 10

Special abilities: Languages, strategy

Malibu is the calm and reliable older twin brother of Kokomo, both of whom are featured in the anime. Fluent in several languages and adept at strategic planning, Malibu is the brains of Team Twin Star. Perhaps because of his high intelligence, he is prone to manipulating not only Kokomo and the Angel Troupe, but also Major Mary. But he's still only a kid, and can't resist the temptation of snacks.

THE NEWLYWEDS
KANAN
FORTE BECAME A MAN...
...AND MARRIED RANPHA.
Forced into it.
HONEY-MOON
Howwww!!!
DARLING... ♡
TROUBLE IN PARADISE
TOUCH ME AND I'LL BLOW YOUR BRAINS OUT!
Huh? Why?

ぱたぱた
PITTER PATTER
Couldn't sleep at all last night.
ALRIGHT, I'M OFF TO WORK.
DARLING, WAIT!

YOUR NECK-TIE'S ...
... CROOKED.

Huh? Why?
DON'T WORRY ABOUT IT.

IF THIS KEEPS UP...
...I'M GONNA LOSE MY MIND.
It's already lost.

HUH? WHAT'S THIS?
RUSTLE

LOVE, RAN-PHA.
FOR MY DARLING.

Swimsuit glamour shots!?
!!!
WHAT GIVES?
キャ
OH!
Tee hee
THEY'RE GOOD LUCK CHARMS...

MINT DECIDES TO TACKLE RANPHA.
HERE I GO.
AAA AAA GH!

MINT ALSO BECAME A MAN.
I have changed.
男
GUY

WHA...
WHAT ARE YOU DOING!!??

WHY ARE YOU STILL IN GIRL CLOTHES?
That skirt looks a bit odd.
BECAUSE ...

...THEY ARE CONVE-NIENT...
...IN VARIOUS WAYS.

SIGH!?
SIGH
URGH! HOW OBNOXIOUS!
Get off of me at once!

VARIOUS?
VARIOUS.
?

ガシャアッ
KA-DAAA
HOLD IT !!
STEP AWAY...
...FROM RANPHA!
じーん...
TOUCHED
DAR-LING!!
DARLING !!!!
DON'T TOUCH ME!
うがーッ
URRGGG..!
The End.
Newlywed #2
Grandpa
Newlywed #3

The G.A. Guide to Financial Planning
Misaki
ALL WE HAVE TO DO IS GET THIS MONEY TO TRANSBAAL BANK.
I'M GLAD THIS IS AN EASY MISSION. ♪
SHEESH, DO THEY THINK THE EMBLEM FRAMES ARE A COURIER SERVICE?
LET'S TAKE ANOTHER PEEK! I'LL PUT IT ON SCREEN!
DON'T BE SO GROUCHY. IT'S NOT EVERYDAY WE SEE ENOUGH MONEY TO BUY A GALAXY.
CLICK
ぱかっ
OPEN
OOPS, THAT BUTTON OPENS THE HATCH!
ひゅ
WWOOOOOSSHH!
MY CALCULATIONS SHOW A 0.0% CHANCE OF RECOVERING THE MONEY.
LOOKS LIKE THE ANGEL TROUPE WILL FINALLY GET THEIR COURT MARTIAL.

NO PROBLEM!
THE ANGEL TROUPE IS ALREADY ACTING UP! WORST CASE SCENARIO, THEY WILL ACCUSE YOU OF LARCENY AND DISSOLVE THE ANGEL TROUPE...
WE'LL JUST HAVE TO RAISE ENOUGH TO COVER THE LOSS!
SQUISH

YOU MAKE IT SOUND EASY, BUT...
Right, Milfeulle?
IT'S A BIG UNIVERSE. THERE SHOULD BE LOTS OF WAYS TO MAKE MONEY.

HOW ABOUT THIS? KIRIKAMURO'S GANG OF SPACE PIRATES, IS WANTED FOR A HUGE REWARD.
THAT'S IT!
SHOOM
SWISH
FORTE, YOU CAN'T DO IT ALONE!

I GOT YOU NOW! CHA-CHING!!
WHAT THE...!?

相討ち STALE MATE

ALAS, SWEET FORTE, YOU BECAME A STAR!
YOUR DEATH WAS NOT IN VAIN!
WE HAVE ACQUIRED 20% OF THE ORIGINAL SUM.
LET US PRAY FOR HER SOUL'S JOURNEY.
CRUEL, CRUEL WORLD.

TO MAKE MONEY... WE NEED TO USE YOUR GOOD LUCK, MILFIE-SAN.
HUH? ME?
THE BEST WAY TO TURN LUCK INTO PROFIT IS...
...GAMBLING!
WITH YOUR LUCK AND MY SPEED-ENHANCED HORSE SUIT, WE CANNOT LOSE!
Acceleration Booster
COMING UP FROM THE SIDE IS SEABISCUIT BLANCMANCHE. SEABISCUIT BLANCMANCHE...
HOORAY!
HOORAY!
HOORAY!
...WINS IT IN A WALK!
THE MOST SUPERB RACE-HORSE IN A HUNDRED YEARS!
NO DOUBT ABOUT IT, THIS HORSE WILL WIN THIS YEAR'S TRIPLE CROWN!!
HUH?
WA- WAIT!
WE'LL PUT YOU OUT TO STUD!
NO, OURS!
PLEASE JOIN US!
WAIT, I AM NOT A HORSE...
HEEEELP!!
ALAS, SWEET MINT, YOU FETCHED A HIGH PRICE AT AUCTION.
HEY! DON'T FORGET TO EAT WELL!
GOOD DEAL!
SO, THEY SELL THEIR COMRADE FOR A QUICK PROFIT...
...DONA DONA...

shoop
VANILLA... WHAT ARE YOU...?
NORMAD IS NOT FOR SALE.
WHAT'S THAT NORMAD, YOU WANT TO BE SOLD TOO?
N-NO, DON'T BE ABSURD!
SHE FLIPPED OUT AND STARTED PREACHING!!
RANPHA CORNERED HER AND NOW LOOK!
THE LAND OF GOD IS CALLING.
IF YOU'RE NOT GOING TO SELL HIM, YOU'D BETTER HAVE A PLAN!
Yes, yes, donate here!
A-HA! SO SHE'S POCKETING THE DONATIONS, EH? I GET IT NOW!
!
BEHOLD, I HAVE HAD A DIVINE VISION!
VANILLA... BETRAYING YOUR FAITH JUST FOR ME...
PLEASE ACCEPT THIS, PRIESTESS VANILLA!
WE MUST BEGIN OUR JOURNEY TO THE PROMISED LAND.
MONEY WILL BE NEEDED FOR THIS JOURNEY.
THE SACRED VIRGIN!
THE CHILD OF GOD!
THE TIME HAS COME, THE DOOR SHALL OPEN...
HUZZOH
MY LITTLE LOST SHEEP, FOLLOW ME!
Ohh, follow the sacred virgin!
HUZZOH
ALAS, SWEET VANILLA, YOU HAVE GONE TO A FAR BETTER PLACE!
WHAT? THIS WASN'T FOR ME, VANILLA?
WAIT! DON'T LEAVE ME!!
SHE HAS FULFILLED HER DESTINY. LET HER GO.
BESIDES, WE GOT WHAT WE WANTED...
shuffle shuffle

WE'RE STILL A LITTLE SHORT.
LOOKS LIKE IT'S MY TURN!
DON'T DO ANYTHING RECKLESS; WE'RE THE ONLY ONES LEFT!
THAT SEEMS TO BE MOSTLY RANPHA'S FAULT.
WHATEVER, WE'LL BE FINE! I HAVE JUST ONE TALENT, AND THIS IS IT!
TKO'D!
RING
HOORAY!
RING
RING
Galactic Martial Arts Tournament.
HOORAY!
THE GRAND CHAMPION IS RANPHA FRANBOISE!
THE WINNER GETS THE TITLE OF "GALAXY'S STRONGEST" AND 100,000 GYARA!
CONGRATULATIONS, CHAMPION RANPHA!
FLASH
HOW DO YOU FEEL NOW THAT YOU ARE THE STRONGEST IN THE UNIVERSE AND WEALTHY ENOUGH TO SLACK OFF FOR THE REST OF YOUR LIFE?
...
NOW THAT I THINK ABOUT IT, I DON'T NEED TO BE IN THE ANGEL TROUPE ANYMORE.
LATER! HAVE FUN, MILFEULLE!
ALAS, SWEET RANPHA, YOU HAVE GONE TO WHERE HAPPINESS LIES!
I'M NOT SURPRISED, GIVEN HER PERSONALITY...
AND THIS STORY...

ANGEL TROUPE, THANKS FOR TRANSPORTING THE DECOY BILLS. ♡
?
WHAT DO YOU MEAN "DECOY BILLS?"
HMM... BEATS ME.
Retire Early!
TEAM TWIN STAR IS HERE TO DELIVER THE CARGO.
TO PROTECT IT FROM PIRATES, WE CARRIED THE REAL CASH, WHILE GIVING YOU COUNTERFEITS.
WE DIDN'T KNOW! HOW CRUEL!
TWINKLE
THAT INFORMATION WAS ONLY DISPERSED ON A "NEED-TO-KNOW" BASIS.
HEH, SENIOR COMMAND KNOWS BETTER THAN TO TRUST YOUR GROUP WITH SOMETHING SO VITAL.
SHIIII III IIIIING
IT IS SAID THAT TO TRICK YOUR ENEMY YOU MUST FIRST TRICK YOUR FRIEND.
HUH?
THAT'S RIDICULOUS!!!
UNLEASH HELL!
FORTE, YOU'RE ALIVE!
ARR GRR HGG URRRH!
KABOOM!
THAT DOES NOT HURT AS MUCH AS BEING SOLD!
MINT, YOU'RE SAFE!
BA-BOOM!
SPARK
WHOOSH
GYAAAAA
BLAM BLAM BLAM
GOD WILL NOT FORGIVE YOU.
I'VE NEVER LIKED YOU, JERKS!
YAY! THE ANGEL TROUPE IS REUNITED!
BEHOLD THE TRUE POWER OF THE EMBLEM FRAMES.
END

WHO IS YOUR FAVORITE "GALAXY ANGEL" CHARACTER?

I know I'm supposed to pick which character I like most, but...

...I love them all.

♥

Look! Milfeulle has combined with Forte! ♥

by かなん

KANAN

WHO IS YOUR FAVORITE "GALAXY ANGEL" CHARACTER?

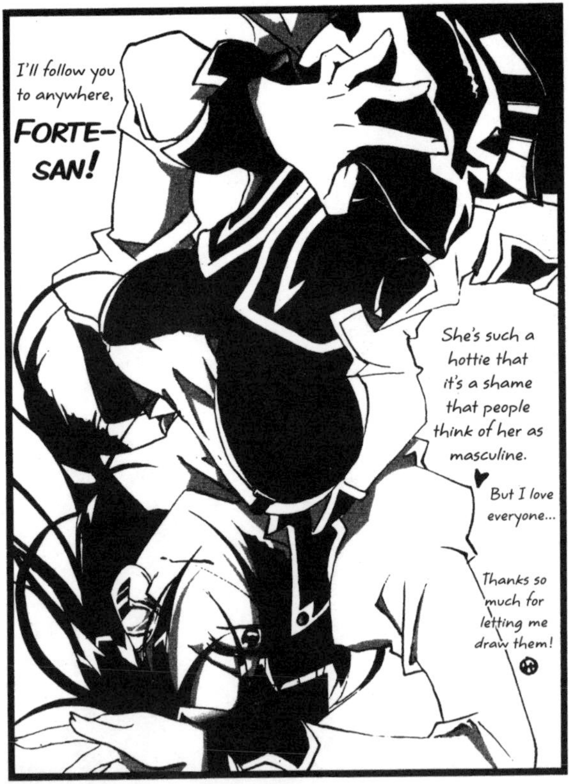

MISAKI

て
PITTER
てく
PATTER
く
AH... VANILLA...
BEING EMBRACED LIKE THIS...
...GIVES THIS LITTLE NORMAD UTTER BLISS.
STOPS
WHAT'S WRONG? VANILLA?
THE TWO NORMADS・・・・・・
GUY NAKAHIRA
THUMP
THUMP

Ta-Da!!

OH!

VANILLA-SAN!

WHAT DO YOU THINK?

WHAT DO I THINK!?

HOW DARE YOU REPLICATE MY VISAGE IN CHEAP COSTUME FORMAT! I'M SPEECHLESS!

WOULD YOU LIKE A RIDE?

HAHAHA! WHAT MADNESS IS THIS!?

SUCH CHICANERY HOLDS NO ALLURE FOR VANILLA!!

DOINK

!?

WA- WAIT, VANILLA!!
THAT IS BUT A THIRD-RATE COUNTER-FEIT!
VANILLA... VANILLA!!

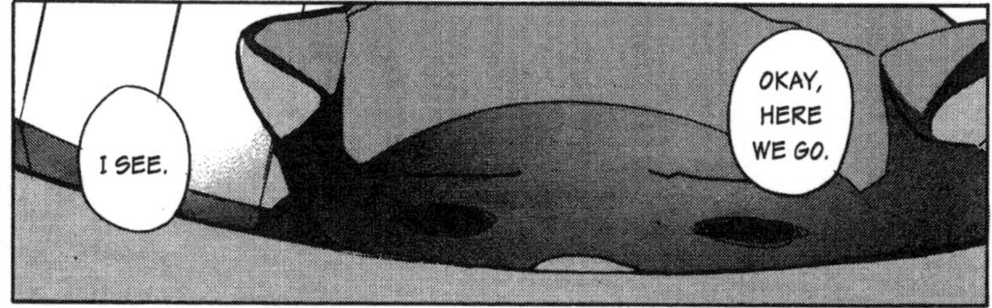
OKAY, HERE WE GO.
I SEE.

OHH...

M-MY VANILLA HAS...

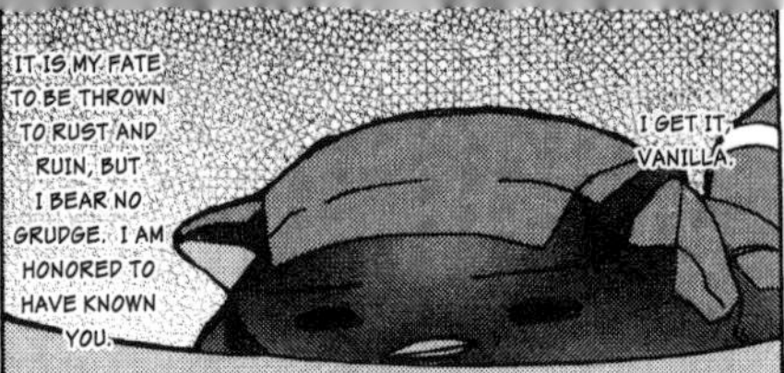

SPARKLE

VA...

VANILLA...

UMMM...

TRASH

THUMP

THUMP

● END ●

Today's Menu:

Ketchup on Fortune Cookies

by: Botan Hanayashiki

WOW! ♥
IS THAT A FORTUNE COOKIE!?
LOOKS YUMMY!
WHAT'S A FORTUNE COOKIE?
YOU DON'T KNOW? IT'S A CHINESE SNACK WITH A NOTE ABOUT YOUR FUTURE INSIDE.
GIRLS LOVE THEM. ♥
crack
LUCKY ME! "GOOD FORTUNE." IT SAYS THAT I'LL FIND SOMETHING I'VE LOST. ♥
OHH ...
SWEET! I WANT IN ON THIS! ♥
crack
...
WHAT DID YOU GET?
GREAT MISFORTUNE
CANNED...
...WHAT'S IT WORTH...
...WHEN DRENCHED IN RED?

THIS IS HOOORRIBLE!
WHIMPER
"RED?" MEANING BLOOD?
WHO THE HECK BROUGHT US THIS EVIL OMEN CRAP!?
NOT ME!
IT WAS ME.
THEY WERE ON THE FLOOR.
HUH?
VANILLA IS NOT TO BLAME.
WE JUST PUT THE COOKIES THERE. YOU'RE THE FOOLS FOR EATING THEM.
...
YOU COULD'VE TOLD US THAT BEFORE WE SCARFED 'EM!
Aaarrgh!

WHIRRR
YEAH, I KNOW I PUT THEM HERE...
...BUT THEY'RE GONE.
YOU THERE!
FLINCH!
DID YOU EAT THE LOST TECHNOLOGY WE DISCOVERED!?
PHEW... YOU HAVE A LOT OF GUTS EATING SOMETHING OFF THE FLOOR.

WE... WE COULDN'T HELP IT, OKAY!?
WE DIDN'T KNOW WHERE THEY CAME FROM!
SO, WHAT'S GONNA HAPPEN TO US!?
I'M SCARED...

THOSE WERE COOKIES THAT TELL FORTUNES... AND THEY ALWAYS COME TRUE!
ALWAYS!?
GOH!
Groovy! I'll find what I lost!

IT GOES LIKE THIS.
THOSE COOKIES DON'T PREDICT. THEY CAUSE WHAT IS WRITTEN TO OCCUR.
"GREAT MISFORTUNE" COOKIE IS LIKE A CURSE.
AT ANY RATE, THIS WILL HAVE TO BE REPORTED...
OH NO YOU DON'T!
TIE UP!

WILL I REALLY BE SOAKED WITH BLOOD!?

SOB!

NO, VANILLA WOULDN'T CURSE PEOPLE.

I SWEAR TO HIS HOLINESS.

DOINK

I HAVE AN IDEA!

HOW ABOUT THIS?

UMMM...
NO! LET ME GO!
COME ON, CUTIE. ♥
HEH
HEH
HEH
SILENCE!
BE A GOOD GIRL AND THIS'LL BE OVER QUICK.
MMM...

No!
HELP ME, MINT!
QUICKLY NOW... OPEN YOUR MOUTH.
I CANNOT.
THIS LAXATIVE MIGHT FLUSH OUT THE FORTUNE COOKIE'S CURSE!
OHOHOHOHO!
HAHAHAHAHA
URK
Phew, I sure feel safer.
Hee hee hee
...
WRIGGLE
WRIGGLE

MINT! RANPHA! FORTE!!
MY TUMMY AND TUSH HURT...
I CAN'T LEAVE THE TOILET!
Boo hoo
Boo hoo
Boo hoo
Boo hoo
TOILET
AWW, POOR GIRL.
SHE HAS BEEN IN THERE FOR THREE HOURS.
WE HAD NO CHOICE, NORMAD.
...
SHE IS CANNED.
SHOCK!
EH, UH...
JUST AS I THOUGHT... IT IS LOST TECH-NOLOGY!
HOW FRIGHT-ENING!
THIS CALLS FOR MORE LAXATIVE!!
WHAT?!

よれ wobble
YOU ARE ALL SO MEAN.
I CAN'T EVEN STAND UP.
よれ wobble
THE EFFECT SHOULD SURELY HAVE PASSED BY NOW.
Good... Good
hee hee hee
YOU WERE LUCKY. RIGHT, MILFEULLE?
YOU AVOIDED THE BLOODBATH.
OH!
WHAT'S THIS WORTH?

OH
!!!
NO!
SHE'S NOT IN THE CLEAR YET!
!
THAT'S THE RED TOPAZ I LOST!
IT'S VERY EXPENSIVE! ♥ ♥
YEAH!!
I CAN'T BELIEVE IT! THE FORTUNE CAME TRUE! ♥
SNATCH
POOF
GOOD FORTUNE
Fortune complete.

NO WAY, IT'S ALL COMING TRUE.

cry

I KNEW IT...

I'M GONNA DIE A HORRIBLE, BLOODY DEATH!

cry

...

Hey, it didn't say you'd die.

WAAH! WAAH!

There, there...

What shall we do?

Vvoot

WHAT'S THAT!?

WOOSH

Vvoot

Angel Troupe, you are ordered to deliver the Lost Technology immediately.

Angel Troupe, move out!

WHAT ARE WE GONNA DO? IF MILFEULLE DIES...
DON'T SAY THAT!
MILFEULLE, YOU WAIT HERE, OKAY?
NO...I'M GOING, TOO.
IF I AM CURSED, IT CAN'T BE HELPED.
I SHOULD NEVER HAVE EATEN THAT COOKIE.
BESIDES ...

...THIS IS MY JOB!

MILFIE!!

STARE

...

SPLORT!

ACK!

BLECH!
eeeewww
WHAT ARE YOU DOING, VANILLA?
THE FORTUNE IS FULFILLED!
HOW?
GREAT MISFORTUNE
CANNED...
POOF
I SEE! "DRENCHED IN RED!"
IT NEVER SPECIFIED WHAT KIND OF RED!
I SEE.
YOU DID IT, VANILLA!!

FATE IS NOT UNKNOWABLE, IF YOU CHOOSE IT YOURSELF.
A-HA!
YES!
ALRIGHT, LET'S GO!!
YAY!
ANGEL TROUPE, MOVE OUT!!
In the end, I think...
Huh?
...that the troupe caused all of my misfortune.

END

WHO IS YOUR FAVORITE "GALAXY ANGEL" CHARACTER?

蘭花さん,
萌へ〜。

RANPHA MAKES ME GO ALL GOOEY.

EVEN THOUGH I DIDN'T DRAW HER IN MY SECTION, I REALLY LOVE RANPHA, ESPECIALLY IN THE GAME AND MANGA. IF I EVER HAVE THE CHANCE, I'LL DRAW HER NEXT TIME!

中平 凱

GUY NAKAHIRA

GALAXY ANGEL™

WHO IS YOUR FAVORITE "GALAXY ANGEL" CHARACTER?

I love Forte. ♡

Her voice, especially...

But my kids:

Hey Mom, why does Forte have such big boobs if he's a man?

???

What!?

Really!?

?

Maybe because she's a woman?

BOTAN HANAYASHIKI

THE ANGEL CAKE COVER-UP
KAZUKI☆SHU
IT'S...
...IT'S GONE!
ふぇえええん
SOB
SOB
SOB
Waaah!
WHAT'S WRONG, MILFEULLE?
MY CAKE DISAPPEARED.
DO ANY OF YOU KNOW WHERE IT WENT?

RANPHA?
HMM, I HAVE NO IDEA.
MINT?
I DO NOT KNOW, EITHER.
FORTE?
ARE YOU SURE YOU MADE A CAKE?
VANILLA?
HOW RUDE! ARE YOU IMPLYING THAT VANILLA PILFERED YOUR PASTRY?
EVERYBODY KNOWS THAT SWEET, GENTLE VANILLA WOULD NEVER COMMIT SUCH A CRIME. YOU ARE QUITE RUDE.
I DIDN'T SAY THAT!
Waaah!
Waaah!
IT VANISHED WHILE I WAS GETTING TEA! I WAS PREPARING IT FOR ALL OF US TO EAT!
GUILT
STAB!
STAB!
STAB!

HEY, MILFEULLE, WE'LL FIND IT FOR YOU.
BUT...
IN THE MEANTIME, HOW ABOUT SOME FRESH TEA?
Y-YEAH, YOU MAKE SUCH DELICIOUS TEA.

OH...WE'RE OUT OF THAT BRAND, SO I'LL HAVE TO GET MORE.
UMM,
Y-YOU KNOW, I'D LIKE SOME OF THAT TEA, TOO!

SWOOSH
OKAY, I'LL BUY SOME. BE RIGHT BACK!
ALRIGHT!
WE GOTTA BAKE A REPLACE-MENT CAKE BEFORE SHE GETS BACK!
Whisper

DASH
BUT FIRST... DESTROY THE EVIDENCE!

EAT ME
...
LOOKS VERY SUSPICIOUS...
IT SEEMS SAFE ENOUGH.
WOW
GROWL
GROWL
EAT ME
TRY A PIECE?
!?
IT'S OKAY. DOESN'T IT LOOK YUMMY?
Y-YEAH, IT DOES BUT...

HERE YOU GO. ♡
むぐ GULP
もぐ CHOMP
もぐ CHOMP
く GULP
ほわ MMMMM
WAS IT GOOD?
NOD
NOD
THAT'S GOOD.
IF IT HAD BEEN POISONED...
...AT LEAST YOU WOULD'VE DIED EATING SOMETHING NICE, YOU KNOW?
SHOCK
...
Just kidding...It was a big "if," even if there was a small chance.
!!!
SHAKE
SHAKE

BY THE WAY...
...DOES ANYONE HERE KNOW HOW TO BAKE?
I CANNOT BELIEVE HOW USELESS YOU ARE.
SHAKE
ふる
SHAKE
ふる
WHAT ABOUT YOU?
CHEAT SHEET.
GOOD THINKING, VANILLA!
ALRIGHT! LET'S GET TO WORK!
CHEAT SHEET
THAT'S MY VANILLA! YOU COULD ALL LEARN A THING OR TWO FROM VANI...
FIRST, POUR THE WHEAT FLOUR INTO THE SIFTER...
WHY SIFT?
IT'S ALL GETTING MIXED TOGETHER ANYWAY!
LUMP
どさっ
LUMP
どさっ

NEXT, THE BAKING POWDER...
HUH? WHICH ONE?
THE SPICIER THE BETTER. ♡
Chili Pepper
TABASCO
FLOP
FLOP
DUNK
!!
Baking Powder
DUNK
IT HELPS POOF IT UP.
SUGAR
LUMP
LUMP
Four dimensional
RANPHA-SAN, WHAT ARE YOU DOING!?
IT WILL BE FAR TOO SWEET WITH THAT MUCH SUGAR!
CAKES ARE SUPPOSED TO BE SWEET!!
HMM... MORE SUGAR!
Then we'll add some caramel, honey, and chocolate...
CAN WE SUBSTITUTE CROCODILE EGGS?
ALRIGHT! A FIFTH OF BOOZE TO FINISH IT OFF.
HUH? CAN WE USE JAPANESE SAKE?
AND NEXT...

OK!

TA-

DA

DONE!

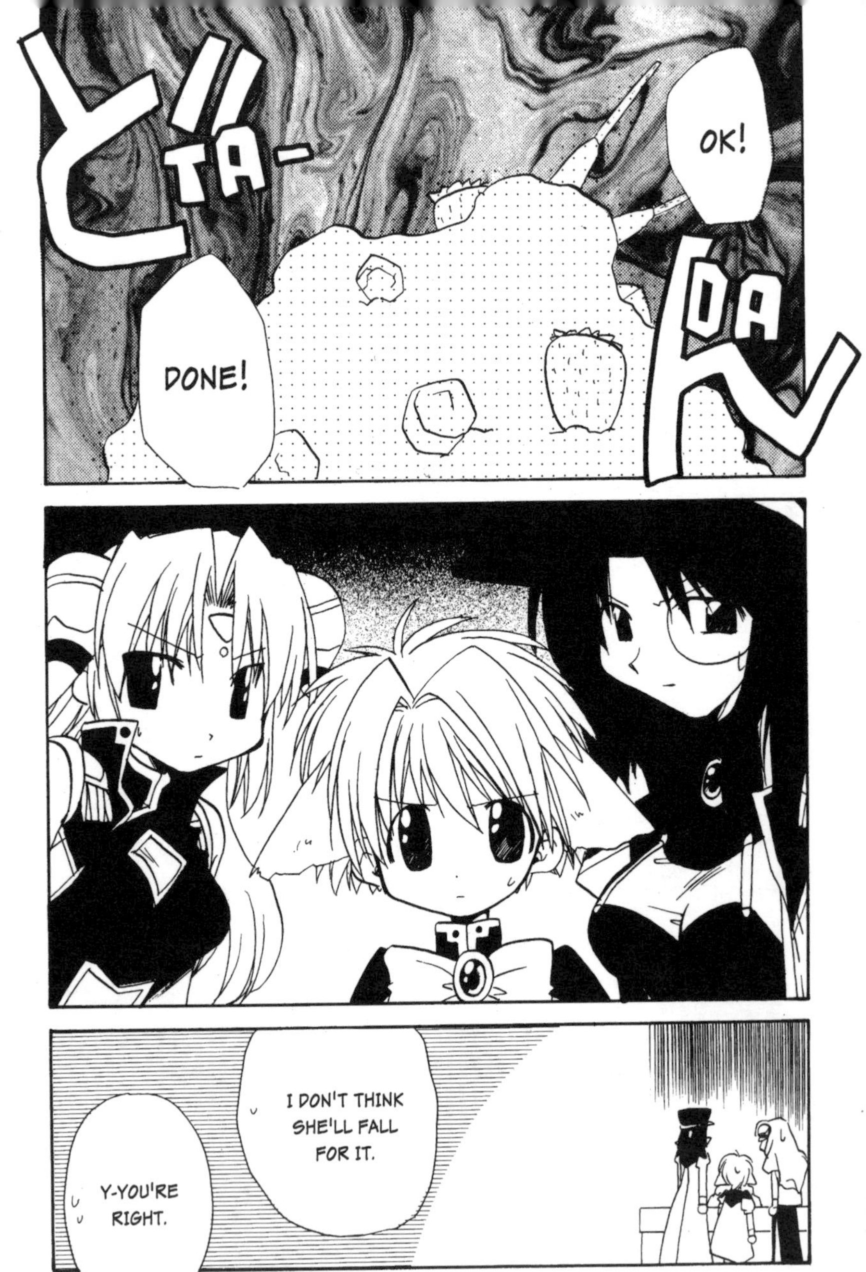

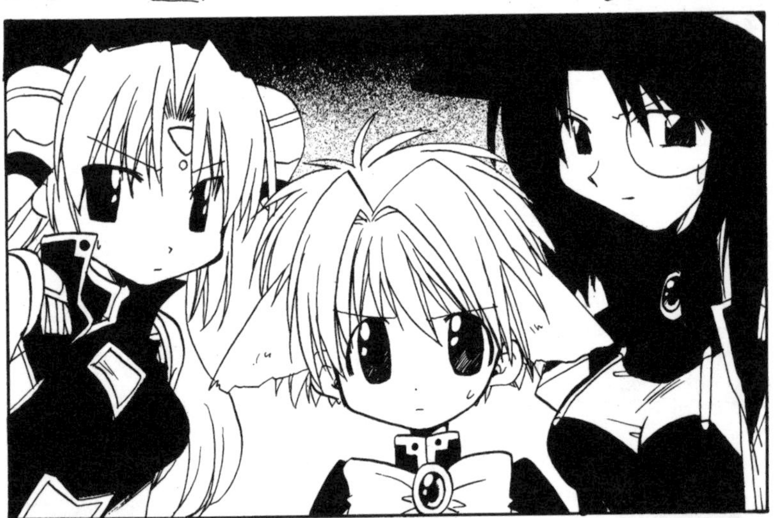

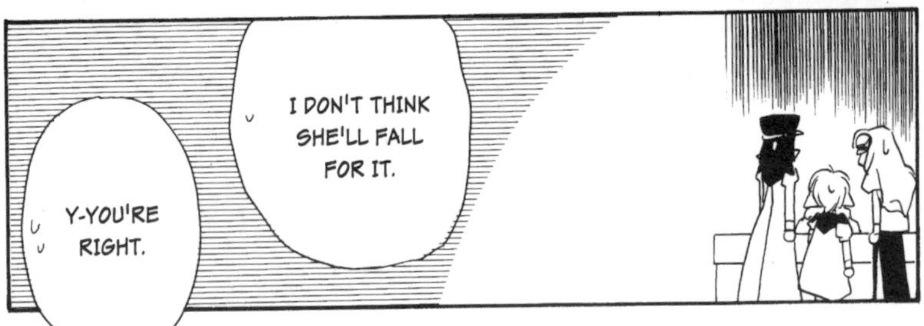

I DON'T THINK SHE'LL FALL FOR IT.
Y-YOU'RE RIGHT.

I'M HOME!
GASP
WELCOME HOME, MILFEULLE!
UMM... ABOUT YOUR CAKE...
Hide Hide
OH, ACTUALLY...
...I FOUND A BUNCH OF GREAT INGREDIENTS WHILE I WAS OUT, SO I'M GONNA MAKE A BRAND NEW ONE! ♡

I'LL GO MAKE IT RIGHT AWAY!

...STEADY... STEADY....

...

DESTROY THE EVIDENCE!

DASH!

•END•

BUBBLE
BUBBLE
Ahhhhh...
IT'S NOT UNUSUAL FOR A BOY...
...TO LIKE LOTS OF GIRLS...
...BUT STILL...
RANPHA'S TROUBLES
蘭花的乙女心
SEARA

WHY...
...AM I SO IRRITATED?

Ack!
ARRGH!!
Exercising didn't relieve the tension!

I KNOW!
SHE MUST BE GETTING...
OH!

IS THAT WHAT IT IS?
RANPHA'S TIME OF THE MONTH?
NO, THAT IS NOT FOR A FEW MORE DAYS.
QUICK REPLY
Hey...
...HOW DO YOU KNOW THAT!?

IT IS MY CLEAR DUTY...
I SEE.

...TO KNOW ABOUT MY COL-LEAGUES. I PAY ATTENTION TO MY SURROUNDINGS...
...AND SEE MANY THINGS.
RUSTLE
YOU DO SCARY THINGS WITH THOSE CUTE EYES.
HEHEHE

THEY SAY "EVERY ROSE HAS ITS THORN," DON'T THEY?
HAHA... THORNS ...EH?
BUT YOU'RE A CACTUS!

IT'S ODD.

I SEE VISIONS OF HIS FACE EVERY-WHERE.

BADUM
BADUM
DOES THIS MEAN I'M IN LOVE?
BADUM
BADUM
WHOOPS, I'VE BEEN CAUGHT!

...
?
ARE YOU REAL?

H...
...HEY, RANPHA.
が
BLUSH
WHA-?
っ

PEEPING? HE'S PEEPING!!
...

ぱっしーん!
WHAP!

HE HAD THAT COMING.
TRULY.

OH!
HERE YOU ALL ARE!

IT'S SNACK TIME!!
SHE'S SO EASYGOING.
MILFIE, YOU'RE STILL WEARING YOUR APRON.
HUH?
OOPS, I FORGOT!
...
HEE HEE!
HERE YOU GO, RANPHA!!
...
munch munch
TODAY I AM A CACTUS.
I WANTED TO BE THORNY, BUT THERE WAS NO BLOWFISH COSTUME.

RANPHA, YOU'VE BEEN SORT OF GLUM LATELY, SO...
...I THOUGHT SOME CALCIUM-FORTIFIED SWEETS WOULD HELP!!
THESE CREAM PUFFS HAVE BEEN STUFFED...
...WITH A HEFTY DOSE OF MILKY CREAM! ♡
MY MOOD WAS MY OWN PROBLEM.
I...
...LIKE HOT THINGS BETTER, YOU KNOW.
OH!
I THOUGHT YOU MIGHT SAY THAT, SO I MADE AN EXTRA SPICY ONE!
This is the hot one.
BUT EVERYONE...
...WAS WORRIED ABOUT ME.
CHOMP!
THAT'S A SWEET ONE, RANPHA.

SWEET STUFF AND CALCIUM, WAS IT? TO CHEER ME UP?
I'M SUCH A FOOL.
THERE ARE THINGS I MUST DO... BEFORE FALLING IN LOVE.
THAT'S WHY...
...I MUST...
...PRETEND THAT I DON'T KNOW MY OWN FEELINGS.
A FEW DAYS LATER
I GAINED TWO POUNDS!
HOW UPSETTING!
Urrg!

● END ●

WHO IS YOUR FAVORITE "GALAXY ANGEL" CHARACTER?

Ranpha and Milfeulle were tied for the lead, until the twins joined the cast.

In other words, I still can't decide. Sigh.

KAZUKI ☆ SHU

WHO IS YOUR FAVORITE "GALAXY ANGEL" CHARACTER?

I love Mint!

Her voice, her personality, her pointy ears, her costumes... She pushes all of my buttons. ♥♥

せあら♥♥
with
ぱすてる

SEARA

Bluer than Indigo

Chisa Mori

AHH, LEMME GUESS, YOU JUST GOT DUMPED.
AS ALWAYS, FORTE UNDERSTANDS.
YEAH, BUT I GAVE HIM A WALLOP!
TEE HEE
FLINCH
DID YOU? GOOD JOB!!
NO WONDER SHE GOT DUMPED.
SO WHY COME TO ME?
WHIRRRR
AAHH!
Close, close, close...
Aahh!
BECAUSE THE OTHERS DON'T UNDERSTAND!
How rude! Right, Vanilla?
Plushie
...
Kid
Oh my...
Big Ears
I'm not stupid!
Stoopid
...
SO?
WHAT DID YOUR HOROSCOPE SAY?
ALTHOUGH SHE'S GRUFF...
...SHE LOOKS AFTER ME.

I CAN ALWAYS RELY ON HER, AND SHE KEEPS AN OPEN MIND.
THAT'S WHY I LIKE HER.
AH!
HERE IT IS!
HOW COULD I GET DUMPED WITH THIS HOROSCOPE!?
I'm frustrated!
AHH!
LET'S SEE.
"YOUR AFFECTION FOR AN IMPORTANT PERSON SHALL DEEPEN."
HMMM...
OKAY.
HUH?
THAT'S ALL?
boing
WHAT?
...
ISN'T THAT GOOD NEWS?
HUH??

THAT'S A WEIRD RESPONSE, COMING FROM YOU.
UH... REALLY?
...
YOU USUALLY TELL ME NOT TO BELIEVE IN "THAT STUPID MUMBO JUMBO!"
Shrug
...
SWISH
YOU WANT CRITICISM!?
snap
MAYBE ...
BUT...
HOW BORING.
Hm?
AWESOME, A NEW GUN!
JUMP
MIND IF I POP OFF A FEW SHOTS? I'M IN BAD MOOD!
Wow!
!!
Heheh
Amazing!
HEY!
PUT THAT DOWN!
OH...
SORRY. THIS GUN IS A LOANER...I'VE BARELY TOUCHED IT MYSELF.
OH, I SEE.

I'M SURPRISED.
FORTE DOESN'T USUALLY...
...YELL LIKE THAT.
THIS GUN MUST BE IMPORTANT TO HER.
HMMPH
Irritated
HOW ODD.
DON'T BE CRUEL!
YEAH, YEAH. I'M SORRY.
I'm tired
Don't say that!
ANYHOW...
WHY'D YOU COME AT A TIME LIKE THIS?
IT'S 4 A.M.!
AFTER ALL...

...YOU DON'T LIKE ME, DO YOU?
Bleh
I ALWAYS LISTEN TO YOUR BABBLING!!
GAH!
You're leaving!?
shoom
FORGET IT!
SHEESH!
tap
tap
SHE ACTS AS IF... THERE'S SOMEONE MORE IMPORTANT THAN ME!
...
TAP
BASED ON HER BEHAVIOR...
...IT SURE SEEMS LIKE SHE DOES!
"PUT THAT DOWN."
AM I SECOND IN LINE?
DOES FORTE HAVE SOMEONE?
I THOUGHT THAT I WAS THE MOST IMPORTANT!
BADUM

HMMM

I DON'T CARE.

WHAT DOES "MOST IMPORTANT" MEAN? THIS ISN'T LIKE ME.
And what's with that "badum?"
EWWW!

I'M MAKING US SOUND LIKE A COUPLE!
twitch

HMMM

HMMM

...FINE BUT...

HMMM

IT'S FINE BUT...

HMMM

HMMM

GOOD MORNING! ♡

HUH?

WHERE'S FORTE?

SHE HAS NOT BEEN HERE.

NOPE! ♡

...

I DON'T KNOW.

DING!

...

I REMEMBERED SOMETHING I NEED TO DO!

DASH

THAT'S IT...IT MUST BE.

SHE WENT TO MEET THE OWNER OF THAT GUN.

HE MUST BE AN IMPORTANT PERSON...SINCE THE GUN IS IMPORTANT TO HER.

IF FORTE IS IN THAT SORT OF RELATIONSHIP...

...SHE WON'T CARE ABOUT ME ANYMORE!!

FORTE!
SHOOM
SWIVEL
SWIVEL
SHE'S NOT HERE.
OH... IT'S HERE.

...
I SHOULDN'T.
I KNOW IT'S WRONG, BUT...
It's light...
SIGH
SHOOM
RANPHA!
FLINCH
AH!
WHAT ARE YOU DOING!?
clank

CLANK

CLANK

OOPS.

WHAT SHOULD I DO?

GASP!
WHO DO YOU THINK YOU ARE?
YOU HAVE GONE TOO FAR. YOU ARE TOTALLY INCONSIDERATE.
EVEN WHEN I TRY TO HELP YOU, YOU ARE THOUGHTLESS.
YOU'RE ANNOYING.

UM.
YOU DON'T CARE ABOUT ME?
?
I SHOULD APOLOGIZE.
...
NNN...
I SHOULD APOLOGIZE.
RIGHT NOW!
SHE HATES ME.

PLOP
WHAT'S WRONG? YOU'RE NOT EATING.
OH...I'M NOT HUNGRY.
Is it?
That's odd.
FORTE ISN'T HERE.
MAYBE SHE WANTS TO BE ALONE.
OH NO.
SHE CAN'T EVEN STAND THE SIGHT OF ME.
I HOPE IT'S NOT TOO LATE FOR US.
SORRY, I'M GOING OUT.
SOB
IT WILL NEVER HAPPEN AGAIN.
SOB
CLICK
SHE CARED FOR IT SO MUCH, BUT I BROKE IT...
I'LL FIX IT, NO MATTER WHAT.
I can't figure it out.
CLICK
SOB
I WANTED TO BE FORTE'S NUMBER ONE.
I don't know anything about guns. -Mori

I NEVER IMAGINED THAT IT'D HURT SO MUCH...
...TO BE WITHOUT FORTE.
I REALLY LIKE HER.
IT LOOKS STRANGE, BUT I THINK IT'S FIXED.
SOB
I SHOULD RETURN THIS AND APOLOGIZE...
...EVEN IF WE WON'T BE THE WAY WE USED TO BE.
OH YEAH, I FORGOT TO ASK WHERE SHE WENT.
THIS IS HOPELESS.
HEY DARLING, ARE YOU ALONE? WANNA HANG OUT?
HUH!?
WHATCHA GOT HERE? LEMME SEE!
GRAB!
GIVE IT BACK!
HEH
TIME TO TEST MY REFLEXES.
YOU THINK YOU CAN BEAT ME!?
GRAB
H- HUH?

WHAT SHOULD I DO?
I MUST BE WEAK FROM SKIPPING MEALS.
THE GUN...
STOP! YOU CAN'T HAVE IT!
WHAM!
LET ME GO!
I'M BEGGING YOU! THIS IS IMPORTANT!
DON'T MESS WITH ME! TRY ANYTHING STUPID, AND I'LL...
UMF!

UMF?

HUH?

FORTE!

YOU LOST TO THIS WIMP?

WHAT ARE YOU DOING HERE?

DID YOU COME TO SAVE ME?

RANPHA.

YOU KNOW THAT TOY GUN?

IS SHE STILL MAD?
SHE ISN'T HERE TO HELP ME...
I'M SORRY!
WEE-OOO
WEE-OOO
WEE-OOO
WHAT?
I WAS SUPPOSED TO RETURN IT TO AN OLD FLAME TODAY.
BUT SOME STRANGE GUY CAME.
MY JEAL-OUSY...
...CAUSED FORTE A LOT OF GRIEF.
M...
...MAYBE HE'LL SHOW UP.
I TRIED TO FIX IT.
IT MIGHT NOT BE COMPLETELY, TOTALLY FIXED.

I HAVE BEHAVED AWFULLY.

I'M AWFUL.

IT'S TRUE. SHE HAS EVERY REASON TO BE ANGRY.

YOU COULD STILL GO SEE HIM.

I WON'T BUG YOU ANYMORE!

shwip

GOOD-BYE!

NAH,

IT'S NOT IMPORTANT.

I SHOULD'VE KNOWN...IT'S A VERY OLD PROMISE.

Something when I was a kid.

FORTE... WHAT ARE YOU SAYING?

BESIDES...

...I KIND OF LIKE YOU.

FORTE.
I MIGHT GET LONELY IF YOU DIDN'T KEEP WHINING TO ME, YOU KNOW?
I DON'T MEAN ANYTHING WEIRD!
ACK!
AND REMEMBER, HOROSCOPES...
Slap
...ARE ALL A SCAM!
"YOUR AFFECTION FOR AN IMPORTANT PERSON SHALL DEEPEN."
NOW, EVEN MORE THAN BEFORE...
OH, I GET IT. IT WAS ABOUT ME!
I FEEL WE ARE CLOSER NOW.
...FORGET IT
RIGHT, RIGHT?
● END ●

DYNAMITE RECIPE
YUZURU ASAHINA
MMM...YUMMY.
HOW CRUEL OF YOU TO EAT A DELICIOUS DESSERT RIGHT IN FRONT OF ME!!
POINT!
That's a felony!
Is it?
AREN'T YOU THE ONE THAT GAVE IT TO ME?

YOU SAID THAT YOU HAD GIVEN UP CAKE...
...SO THAT YOU COULD GET A DYNAMITE BODY LIKE MINE.
YES, BUT IT'S SO CRUEL!!
TA-DA
IF YOU CAN'T CONTROL YOURSELF...
...YOU'LL NEVER LOOK LIKE ME! ♡
OHO HO HO HO HO

WAAAAH!
YOU'RE MEAN!!
THAT'S MY FAVORITE CAKE!
CHOMP
THAT'S THE WAY IT GOES!
AAAHHH!
GRIN
FINE.
SETTLE DOWN!!
GOBBLE
GOBBLE
GOBBLE
!!

GOBBLE
GOBBLE
I'LL JUST EAT EVERYTHING! I'LL JUST EAT EVERYTHING! I'LL JUST EAT EVERYYYYTHING!
NO WAY! CUT IT OUT!!
GULP
GULP
I WAS SAVING THAT ONE FOR LATER!
YOU'RE TOO SLOW!
Buh?!
Gooood mooorning.
How about some tea? Tee hee.
Weeble wobbles!?
BLOP
FINALLY, MIL-FEULLE ACHIEVED HER DREAM OF HAVING THE SAME DYNAMITE BODY AS RANPHA.

END

WHO IS YOUR FAVORITE "GALAXY ANGEL" CHARACTER?

HELLOOOOOOOO!
MORI LIKES RANPHA.
HER AMOROUSNESS AND
NAÏVETÉ ARE ADORABLE.
SHE'S SO CUTE!
THIS PARTICULAR DRAWING
MAKES HER LOOK LIKE A
STUPID SCHOOL GIRL.
(MAYBE SHE IS!) HAHA!
IT'S BEEN FUN DRAWING
SHOJO MANGA. ♡

THANKS SO MUCH!!
I HOPE WE MEET AGAIN, TEE
HEE. SEE YOU,

森ちさ 2003.

CHISA MORI

WHO IS YOUR FAVORITE "GALAXY ANGEL" CHARACTER?

蘭花

RANPHA!!

I LOVE HER BODY (LOL) AND THE WAY THAT SHE'S ALWAYS ON THE BRINK OF LOVE.
NORMAD'S CUTE, TOO...THE NORMAD PUNCHING BAG WAS THE BEST! (LOL)

朝比奈ゆづる MAVERIX

YUZURU ASAHINA

HUH?
WHO IS THAT GUY?
UM...
...EXCUSE ME?
RANPHA-SAN?
THE BEAUTIFUL COSTUME
YUUMA SUZUKA

Don't ask me how she makes the arms and legs work!

I KNEW YOU LIKED COSPLAY...
...BUT I DIDN'T KNOW YOU WERE INTO CROSS-PLAY.
THIS TYPE OF OUTFIT IS EX-TREMELY RARE!
HOW COULD ONE RESIST WEARING IT!?
GRIP
Would you even call that a "costume?"
REGARD-LESS, YOU NEED TO GET OUT OF IT.
I DID SOME RESEARCH, AND...
OH!
RAN-PHA-SAN!
W-WHAT?
PLEASE, PUNCH THE COSTUME IN THE FACE!

UMMM... WHAT!?
THIS LOST TECHNOLOGY GETS WEAKER AS IT GETS UGLIER.
ONCE IT IS WEAKENED, I CAN TAKE IT OFF.
IT SEEMS TO HAVE SOME SORT OF DEFENSE MECHANISM...
...SO I CANNOT PUMMEL IT MYSELF!
I CAN'T DESTROY SOMETHING SO PRETTY!
RA-RANPHA-SAN?
THERE MUST BE ANOTHER WAY TO GET YOU OUT.
TH-THAT HURTS, RANPHA-SAN!
PULL

PL- PLEASE STOP!
RANPHA-SAN!
あっ!!
AH!!!!
HUFF
ハァ
HUFF
ハァ
BADUM
ドッ
キ
BADUM
ドッ
キ
OH—
RAN-PHA-SAN?
WHY NOT JUST STAY IN THERE?
WHAT DO YOU MEAN!?
I'LL TAKE YOU, IF NO ONE ELSE WILL!
きゃっ
yay!
PLEASE DO NOT SAY THAT!

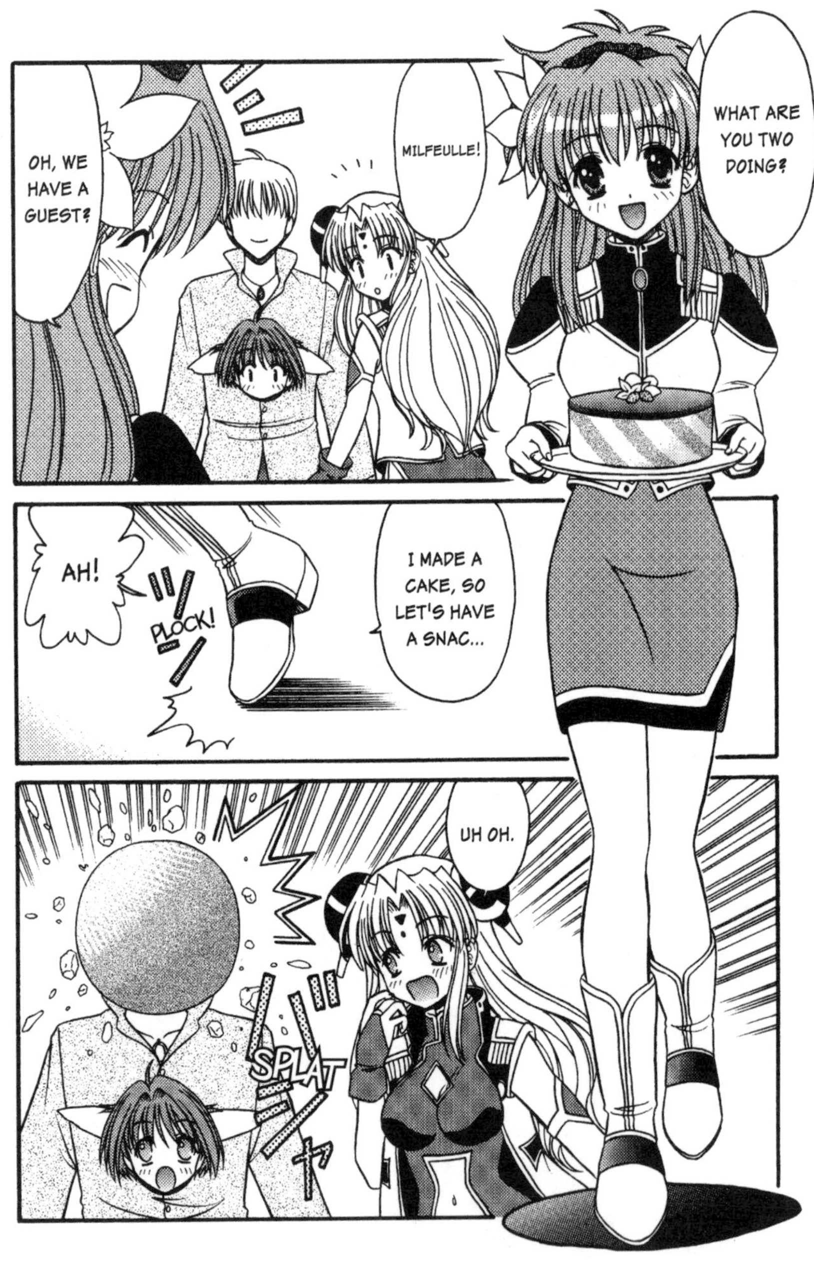
WHAT ARE YOU TWO DOING?
MILFEULLE!
OH, WE HAVE A GUEST?
I MADE A CAKE, SO LET'S HAVE A SNAC...
AH!
PLOCK!
UH OH.
SPLAT

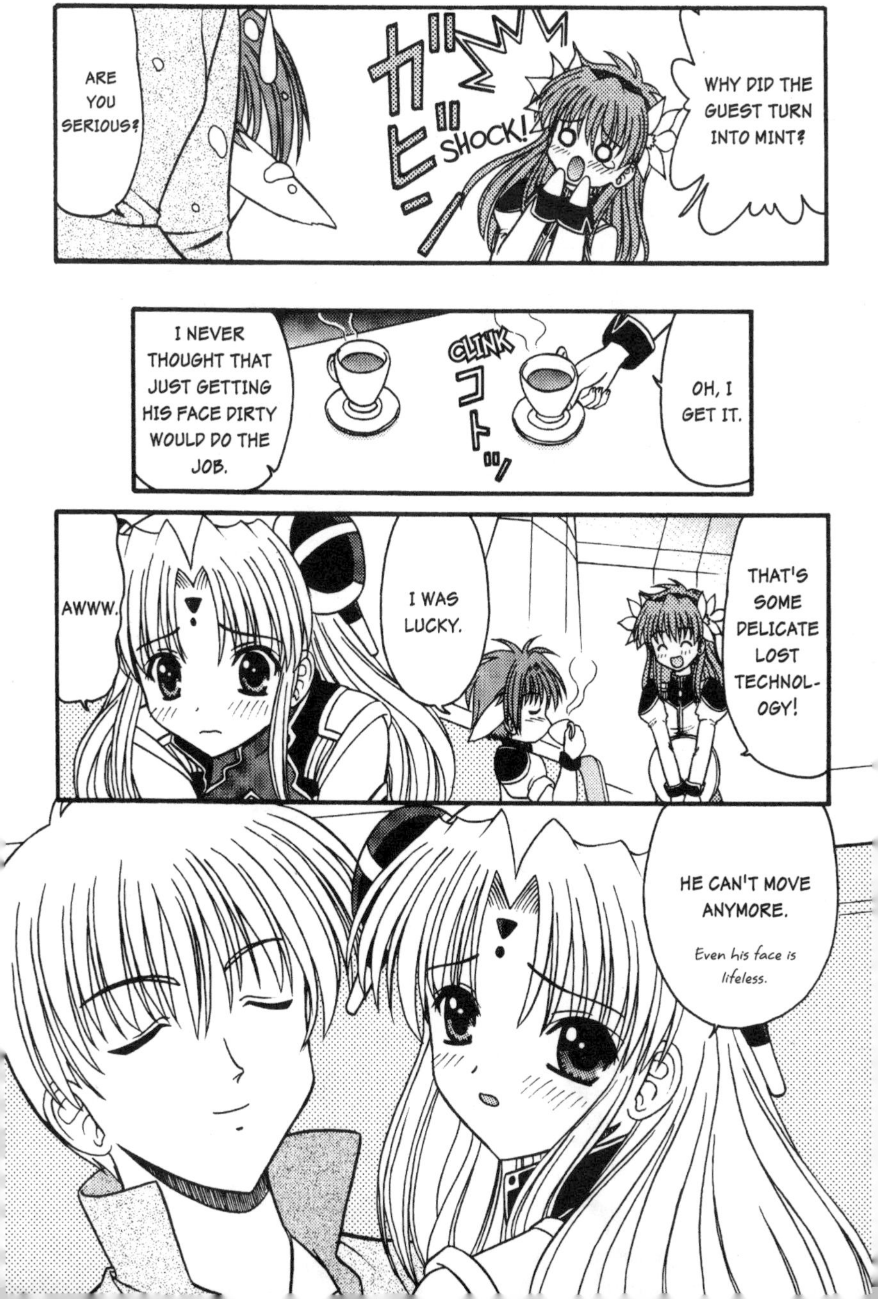

WHY DID THE GUEST TURN INTO MINT?
SHOCK!
ARE YOU SERIOUS?

OH, I GET IT.
CLINK
コトッ
I NEVER THOUGHT THAT JUST GETTING HIS FACE DIRTY WOULD DO THE JOB.

THAT'S SOME DELICATE LOST TECHNOLOGY!

I WAS LUCKY.

AWWW.

HE CAN'T MOVE ANYMORE.

Even his face is lifeless.

OF COURSE. IT IS, AFTER ALL, AN EMPTY COSTUME.

WAAH, MY POOR JAMES!

WAAH

SIGH...

OH, FINE.

WAAH

Since when does it have a name? (LOL)

...

NOW WE HAVE ANOTHER CREWMAN.

Clap Clap Yay

THIS SUCKS!

END

らんらんら～ん♪
La La La
YUMMY, YUMMY CUPCAKES!
I... CAN'T... BREATHE!
RELEASE ...ME!
WHO'S THERE?
OVER.. HERE!
SWISH
SWISH
MIL-FEULLE, HELP!
DIRTY☆NORMAD
BY Kotomi nekoma
BEHIND YOU!
ぎゃあああああ
AAAAAAAGH!

RANPHA DID THIS TO ME!
HOW MEAN!
SHE LEFT ME FOR DEAD IN A TRASHCAN!
IT'S TOO MUCH TO BEAR, I TELL YOU!
OH, DID I DO THAT? I'M SO SORRY.
I GUESS I CONFUSED YOU WITH GARBAGE.
THAT IS NOT HELPING, RANPHA-SAN.
WELL, HE DOES LOOK A LITTLE TRASHY.
And dirty, too.
I WOULD LIKE FOR YOU THREE TO THINK ABOUT SOMETHING.
WHO GOT ME DIRTY?
WHO IS RESPONSIBLE FOR ALL OF MY PAIN AND SUFFERING?
I ACCUSE YOU IDIOTS OF THESE CRIMES!

WEEP
WHEN YOU PUT IT THAT WAY, I FEEL KIND OF SORRY FOR YOU.
WEEP
HMPH!
YOU'RE STILL A FILTHY LITTLE WRETCH, NO MATTER WHAT YOU SAY!
YOU WERE THROWN OUT BECAUSE OF YOUR AWFUL LITTLE BODY!
WHY DON'T YOU JUST GET A NEW ONE AND STOP WHINING?
MAKES SENSE...
THAT'S A GREAT IDEA! ♪
FLINCH!
HEY....
WHAT DO YOU THINK, MINT?
ME?

I...I THINK...
...THAT NORMAD HAS BEEN WRONGED.
よろりっ WOBBL
WE ALL HAVE BIASES ABOUT PEOPLE'S WORTH, THEIR APPEARANCE AND EVEN THEIR RIGHT TO EXIST.
WHO ARE WE TO JUDGE?
OH, MINT!
THAT IS TRUE.
SO TRUE...
I WILL NOT STAND FOR IT!
だっしゅ DASH
WHOA, SLOW DOWN!
SHE'S AT THAT TROUBLED AGE.
HMMM...

THAT WAS A CLOSE ONE.
IF THEY HAD STARTED LOOKING FOR A NEW BODY FOR NORMAD...
...THEY MIGHT HAVE COME AFTER MY COSTUMES!
THE TRUTH
SO...
WHAT'S THE PLAN?
I KNOW!
I HAVE A TERRIFIC IDEA!
WHY DON'T WE JUST WASH HIM?
THAT'S IT!
WHY DIDN'T WE THINK OF THAT BEFORE?
REALLY! ♪
CHUNKA
CHUNKA

LATER...
LOOK AT THAT! HE'S CLEAN AS A WHISTLE!
ACK!
SHREDDED
WE REALLY GOT THE GRIME OUT.
ISN'T HE NICE AND CLEAN?
WE TURNED THE WASHER'S SETTING TO "TYPHOON."
SURE, HE'S CLEAN...
Uhhh...
...BUT NOW HE DOES LOOK LIKE TRASH.
FEELS GREAT, RIGHT NORMAD?
...
CLANK
UH... VANILLA?

WHO IS YOUR FAVORITE "GALAXY ANGEL" CHARACTER?

♥RANPHA♥
I FIND HER CHINESE CLOTHING TO BE ODDLY APPEALING. (LOL)
http://www9.plala.or.jp/process/

YUUMA SUZUKA

WHO IS YOUR FAVORITE "GALAXY ANGEL" CHARACTER?

I LIKE RANPHA MOST OF ALL!
HER VOICE...HER PERSONALITY...HER APPEARANCE...I LOVE THEM ALL!
THE INTERACTION BETWEEN FORTE♪ AND RANPHA IS GREAT, AND SHE WAS SO ADORABLE AS A KID! (> <)

BY猫間ことみ
http://www.aj.wakwak.com/~nekoma/

KOTOMI NEKOMA

はあ…
Sigh...
MINT IN LOVE
Yuu Nanahara
IS SOMETHING WRONG, MILFEULLE?
IT'S MINT.
WHAT'S GOING ON WITH HER?
SHE SURE HAS BEEN SIGHING A LOT.
YEAH, SHE HASN'T BEEN HERSELF LATELY.
I WONDER WHAT'S WRONG.
NO WAY!

IF SHE HAD A PROBLEM SHE WOULD'VE TOLD US!
We're not strangers!
...
MAYBE THOSE ARE REALLY DONKEY EARS.
whisper
...
...
...
King?
COME ON NOW, YOU'RE SUPPOSED TO LAUGH. RIGHT, VANILLA?
Hmmm
I AM FAMILIAR WITH MINT'S SYMPTOMS.
REALLY?
A HEART-BREAKING SIGH...
...DISTANT, UNFOCUSED EYES...
...SLIGHTLY FLUSHED CHEEKS.

YES...
...SHE IS AFFLICTED WITH...
LOVE SICKNESS!
LOVE!?
sickness?
WHAAAAT?
えー…
ARE YOU SERIOUS?
NO DOUBT.
I FALL IN LOVE ALL THE TIME, SO I KNOW.

WELL, I GUESS MINT IS AT THAT AGE...
OH!
EXCUSE ME.
MINT!
O-OKAY.
WHERE ARE YOU GOING?
I WILL BE AWAY FOR A WHILE.
I MUST...
...GO SOMEWHERE TO SORT OUT THESE FEELINGS.

I WILL RETURN SHORTLY.
I TOLD YOU SO, I TOLD YOU SO, I TOLD YOU SO!!
shwip
...
...
...
...
MINT...
MINT, YOU'RE SERIOUS ABOUT THIS, AREN'T YOU?
I'M ROOTING FOR YOU!
Woo hoo!
NOW, LET'S FOLLOW HER!
BAD IDEA, RANPHA!
We shouldn't interfere!

WHERE DO YOU THINK SHE WENT?
Ummm...
SHE MUST BE SOMEWHERE AROUND HERE.
OH!
THERE SHE IS, OVER THERE!
WHERE? WHERE!? WHO'S SHE WITH?
HUH?
THAT GUY WITH MINT IS...
KOKOMO!? WHAT'S HE DOING HERE?
COULD IT BE ...
MINT'S CRUSH...

KOKOMO!?
SHOCK
SIGH
flap
I KNEW IT.
flap
flap
IT IS GLORIOUS.
OKOJO COSTUME
Discount prices!
Buy it today!

THERE ARE ONLY FIVE OF THESE COSTUMES IN THE WHOLE UNIVERSE.

I COULD NEVER AFFORD ONE BEFORE.

IT IS MAGNIFICENTLY CONSTRUCTED.

I CANNOT RESIST! I MUST HAVE IT!

THERE YOU ARE, KOKOMO.

You wandered off again.

MALIBU!

That's it, we're going home.

Welcome!

DRAG ズルズル

ズルズル DRAG

AHHH, I WANNA BUY SOME MODEL KITS!!

BY THE WAY...
...WHY HAVE YOU ALL BEEN ACTING SO ODD LATELY?
WE HAVE?
AHAHAHA
HEY, WHATEVER FLOATS YOUR BOAT.
I'm still rooting for you, Mint!

END

KNOCK KNOCK
YES? ♪
MILFIE-SAN, IS THIS A GOOD TIME?
I HAVE A FAVOR TO ASK OF YOU.
Full of Dreams
Sweet as Cream
Sure to Please
Marshmallow Mint
Hanamaru Togawa

THAT'S NO PROBLEM, MINT!

I'LL WHIP IT UP TOMORROW. ♡

La la la

La DI Da

VANILLA, WHAT IS ALL THIS? MINT IS DISTURBINGLY CHEERFUL.

FWOMP

ポ
POP
とろ〜ん
DREAMY
WOW!
うっとり〜
RAPTURE
IT IS FABULOUS! ♡
ぱぱ〜ん!!
TA-DA!!
NOW, THEN...
WHOMP
I KNEW IT WOULD WORK! THIS MARSH-MALLOW COSTUME IS THE BEST! ♡

IT FITS SO WELL, I JUST CANNOT STAND IT.
FLUFF ふわ FLUFF ふわん
SNIFF SNIFF
WHAT AN OVERWHELM-INGLY SWEET FRAGRANCE!
NUZZLE ほか ふか NUZZLE
IT IS AL-MOST TOO MUCH!! ♡
THIS COSTUME WILL BE GREAT FOR...
poof もこ
poof もこ poof もこ

HAPPY
わく
HAPPY
わく
...WEARING TO BED! ♪
JOY
どき
JOY
どき
I AM SURE IT WILL GIVE ME WONDERFUL DREAMS! ♡
SPARKLE
キラーン
CLICK
OHHH, I AM SO HAPPY!
HEHEHE
フフフ。。

AAAAAHHHH!

FLINCH

HOW!?

MY COSTUME IS GONE!

THIS MUST BE THE WORK OF AN ANGEL TROUPE MEMBER. I WILL FIND THE VILLAIN AND EXPOSE HER.

MINT NEVER LEARNED THE HORRIBLE TRUTH: IN HER MARSHMAL-LOWY SLUMBER, SHE HAD DROOLED ALL OVER HERSELF, DISSOLVING HER SUGARY COSTUME COMPLETELY.

REALLY?
OH, YEAH.

DID ANYONE ELSE JUST FEEL THAT CHILL?

...

END

WHO IS YOUR FAVORITE "GALAXY ANGEL" CHARACTER?

MINT!

Honestly, I just like her looks. (Tee hee)

Y. NANAHARA

YUU NANAHARA

WHO IS YOUR FAVORITE "GALAXY ANGEL" CHARACTER?

My favorites are Milfeulle and Mint.♥

Between Milfeulle's flightiness and Mint's hobbies there is much to love!♥

HANAMARU TOGAWA

Galaxy Home Shopping Network

Akari Kita

THE GALAXY HOME SHOPPING NETWORK ...
...IS BROUGHT TO YOU BY ANIME GAMERS.
Galaxy Home Shopping
DEJIKO AND PUCHIKO HERE...
...TO OFFER YOU SOMETHING VERY SPE-CIAL NYU!
Goodie!
FLAP
FLAP
WHIRR
BLAH
BLAH

ARE THEY SELLING ANYTHING GOOD?
Welcome back, everyone.
LOOK AT THAT CUTE COSTUME. ♡
YES.
HERE'S TODAY'S ULTRA-REPULSIVE ITEM NYO. CHECK IT OUT NYO.
Butter Bean Costume
GHASTLY NYU.
YOU REALLY THINK THAT'S CUTE?
YOUR TASTES ARE TRULY STRANGE...
...JUST LIKE THE LAST COSTUME YOU BOUGHT.
Dejiko calls it "ultra-repulsive."
WHAT!?
HOW COULD YOU NOT THINK IT IS CUTE?
MILFEUILLE-SAN AGREES WITH ME!

ジャーン
TA-DA!
Ummmm
THE ONE YOU JUST BOUGHT?
やかん
TEA POT
I THINK IT'S TERRIFIC!
SEE, IT EVEN HAS A FUNCTIONING SPOUT!
glub glub
IS THAT A GOOD THING?

MINT HAS NOT BEEN CONSTRUCTING HER OWN CUTE COSTUMES LATELY, HAS SHE?
SHE HAS TARNISHED THE TITLE OF COSPLAY CZAR OF CUTENESS!
PERK
WHAT IS THIS "COSPLAY CZAR OF CUTENESS" NONSENSE?
THIS CANNOT STAND!
VERY WELL, THEN!!
I WILL SHOW YOU WHAT IT MEANS TO FEEL THE POWER OF THE GALAXY'S STRONGEST COSPLAY CZAR!
Hey, what the heck is a Cosplay Czar!?

SO...
WHY DID YOU MAKE A COSTUME OF ME?
Made by Mint
WOW! THAT LOOKS PERFECT! ♡
Very nice.
Handmade, eh?
Hohohoho
IN WHAT WAY IS THAT MONSTROSITY ANYTHING RESEMBLING "PERFECT?"
You are all blind!!
I DON'T LOOK EVEN REMOTELY LIKE THAT!

I GIVE UP. YOU IGNORAMUSES, ROWDY, CRUDE AND WITHOUT REFINEMENT, SIMPLY...
...ARE TOO STUPID TO UNDERSTAND ONE SUCH AS ME.
MY DEAR VANILLA, ON THE OTHER HAND...
...DOES NOT UNDERSTAND, EITHER!
VANILLA, CAN YOU NOT SEE THE SIZE DIFFERENCE?
There, there.
HEHE ♡

GRAB
SO, UNLIKE THOSE OF US WHO ARE ROWDY, CRUDE AND UNREFINED...
RUMBLE RUMBLE
GRIP
...YOU THINK THAT YOUR PRECIOUS VANILLA UNDERSTANDS YOU?
!
YOU'LL PAY FOR THAT COMMENT!
CHUCK
WAAAH!
GET LOST!

WHOOOSHHHH!
WHA...
TWINKLE
AAAAAAAH!!!
THE END

VANILLA, MY LOVE ✦ HINA.

CARDIGAN?
GU-AR-DI-AN, VANILLA, GUARDIAN!
I WILL BE YOUR OWN PERSONAL BENEFICENT DEITY!
I WILL SACRIFICE EVERYTHING FOR YOU, INCLUDING MY MORTAL LIFE!
I WILL RAIN HAPPINESS UPON YOU, BRING YOU FAME AND FORTUNE, TRANSUBSTANTIATE YOU INTO A GODDESS!
SIM HEAVEN

ARGH! A SPACE COCKROACH!
SCUTTLE
SCUTTLE
SCUTTLE

STARE
STARTLED

VANILLA, PLEASE STOP!

SPACE COCKROACHES ARE MY ONE AND ONLY PHOBIA!

I CAN PROTECT YOU FROM ANYTHING BUT THAT!

CREEP

FLAP

FLAP

FLAP

HEY!

WHAT DO YOU HAVE THERE, VANILLA?

A GUARDIAN.
HUH? ACCORDION?
SPACE MOUSE.
SQUEAK
KEEP IT AWAY, VANILLA!
SPACE MICE ARE MY ONE AND ONLY PHOBIA!
HEY, RANPHA...
...IS AN ACCORDION SOMETHING THAT YOU WEAR ON YOUR HEAD?
PFFFFFT
Ahhh... bored.
Isn't there anything to do?
END

WHO IS YOUR FAVORITE "GALAXY ANGEL" CHARACTER?

My favorite character is

NORMAD

Even though he's a specimen of the precious Lost Technology, the Angel Troupe gives him absolutely no respect!
Even though he is shot, torn up, taped back together and has his stuffing eaten, he still gives his wholehearted, unrequited love to Vanilla (although perhaps it is mutual?)!
When Vanilla holds him, he looks so funny with her hair on his head!

Arrogant!

Of course you like me, although I don't like your rationale.

Normad's true form!

?!

来多あかりでした。

http://members.jcom.home.ne.jp/kitaakari/

AKARI KITA

WHO IS YOUR FAVORITE "GALAXY ANGEL" CHARACTER?

Normad is cool because he's so verbose.

ひな。

HINA.

AAAAH!
THUNK
JEEZ...
...WHAT'S GOING ON HERE?
FLUTTER
OWWWW.
I'll get it... jeez.
Sorry!
...
!
UH OH.
Mint's Technicolor Curry ♡
by: Chata Tachibana

OH MY GOSH!

YOU HAVE A TERRIBLE FEVER!

HUH? I DON'T THINK SO.

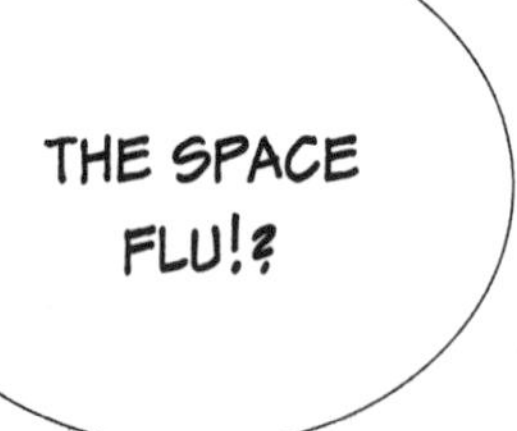

WITH SOME REST, YOU SHOULD BE BETTER IN A FEW DAYS.
JUST TAKE YOUR MEDICINE AND STAY IN BED.
YES, DOCTOR.
SHWIP!
YOU REALLY HAD US WORRIED.
I CAN'T BELIEVE IT'S SPACE FLU.
I AM NOT SURPRISED.
LUGGING YOU OVER HERE WAS NO EASY TASK!
THANKS FOR HELPING ME, RANPHA.
THERE WAS A LOT OF IT GOING AROUND ON THE LAST PLANET WE VISITED.

AN EXTRATERRESTRIAL GERM?

WELL, ANYWAY...

...JUST TAKE YOUR MEDICINE AND GET SOME REST. DON'T WORRY ABOUT A THING, MILFEULLE.

OKAY.

BUT...
...WHAT SHOULD I DO...

...ABOUT TONIGHT'S DINNER?
?
YOU...

BUT MILFIE-SAN HAS A POINT. YOU ALL ARE PROBABLY TOO INCOMPETENT. I WILL COOK.

RANPHA-SAN IS RIGHT.
YOU IDIOT!
WE'RE NOT CHILDREN! WE'LL COOK IT OURSELVES!

I AM LOOKING FORWARD TO IT.

THERE IS THIS ONE THING THAT I HAVE ALWAYS WANTED TO TRY.

I DIDN'T KNOW YOU COULD COOK, MINT.

IT IS NO PROBLEM.

I DON'T LIKE THE SOUND OF THAT...

Milfie-san, would you like some porridge?

Thank you

MINT'S WORDS...
...WERE STRANGELY OMINOUS.
Try?

YOU WORRY TOO MUCH.
BUT, FORTE!
YOU'LL AGE FASTER IF YOU WORRY ABOUT TRIVIALITIES.
WHAT!?
BEEP

I AM SORRY TO KEEP EVERYONE WAITING.
We will have curry for dinner tonight.

WELL, THAT'S GOOD NEWS.
IT WOULD TAKE AMAZING SKILL TO MESS UP CURRY.
TRUE, TRUE.
DID WE KEEP YOU WAITING, MINT?
EVERYONE IS RIGHT ON TIME...
...AND EVERYTHING IS READY.

WOW! LOOKS AWE...

...SOME.

TA-DA!

A DISTURBINGLY BLUE CURRY.

MINT HAS AMAZING SKILL.

MINT?
YES?
IS THIS CURRY?
YES, IT IS.
SHOULD IT BE BLUE?

OH, YES.
ACROSS THE GALAXY THERE ARE RED CURRIES, GREEN CURRIES, YELLOW CURRIES AND WHITE CURRIES...

I LOVE THE BRIGHTNESS OF ARTIFICIAL COLORS!
...SO DOES IT NOT MAKE SENSE TO HAVE A BLUE CURRY, TOO? ♡
NOT REALLY...
Bon apetite...

CHOMP
Ignore the blue.
Ignore the blue.

HOW IS IT?
...

I TASTE SOMETHING OTHER THAN CURRY POWDER.
LIKE WHAT!?

I HAD TO ADD A LOT OF BLUE #30 TO GET RID OF THE NATURAL YELLOW.*
BLUE #30 HAS A FLAVOR!?
chomp

*THE BASE IS CURRY FLAVOR.

IF YOU ADD THIS, YOUR CURRY WILL TURN A PRETTY PURPLE! ♡
THANK GOD SHE CAN'T REACH MINE.
SNAP
PINK FOOD COLORING.
SHAKE
SHAKE
BY THE WAY, MINT...
...DID YOU TAKE MILFIE HER DINNER?
YES, OF COURSE.
sob sob

MILFIE-SAN, I BROUGHT YOU SOME PORRIDGE.
THANK YOU, MINT.
MY PLEASURE. ♡
THIS PORRIDGE IS PINK!
IT MATCHES YOUR HAIR! ♡
WHEN YOU ADD THIS, THE COLOR CHANGES AGAIN!
WOW!
Yellow #4
It's orange now!
Amazing!
Cool!
I am glad that you like it.
THAT IS THE WHOLE STORY.

WHAT COLOR MEALS WOULD YOU ALL LIKE TOMORROW?

I PROMISED HER SOME BLUE PORRIDGE TOMORROW!
WHAT!?

WHAT COLOR!?
Not again!
Color-coded cooking?

WHAT'S WRONG, RANPHA?
sob sob
Your lips are purple.
PLEASE GET WELL... SOON.

END

WHO IS YOUR FAVORITE "GALAXY ANGEL" CHARACTER?

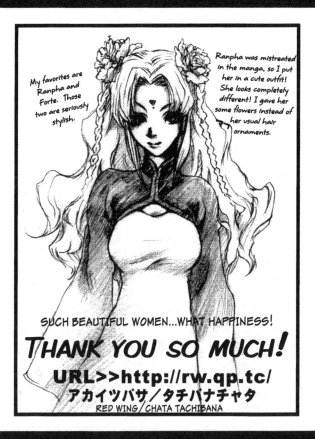

My favorites are Ranpha and Forte. Those two are seriously stylish.

Ranpha was mistreated in the manga, so I put her in a cute outfit! She looks completely different! I gave her some flowers instead of her usual hair ornaments.

SUCH BEAUTIFUL WOMEN...WHAT HAPPINESS!

THANK YOU SO MUCH!

URL>>http://rw.qp.tc/

アカイツバサ／タチバナチャタ

RED WING / CHATA TACHIBANA

CHATA TACHIBANA

Translation Notes

pg. 12 yakitori - A dish of chicken bits grilled on skewers, it is popular with Japanese businessmen.

pg. 12 oden - A type of Japanese food served during the winter. It is a hot pot dish which includes daikon radish, fish cakes, boiled eggs, seaweed, mochi (Japanese rice cake), and other items. In Japan, businessmen often eat dinner at restaurants that serve oden steaming hot.

pg. 25 "...dona dona..." - A reference to a Yiddish song in which a farmer sells off the cow. "Dona dona..." is from the refrain.

pg. 27 gyara - Gyara is the currency in the universe of Galaxy Angel. It is also Japanese for "gig money."

pg. 32 cosplay - Cosplay is a term invented in Japan, joining the two words "costume" and "play." It usually refers to a person who dresses up as a character from an anime or game.

pg. 59 sake - Japanese wine brewed from rice.

pg. 116 donkey ears - A reference to the story of King Midas, also famous for his golden touch.

pg. 129 okojo costume - Okojo is a Japanese ermine, and member of the weasel family. Its coat is usually and orange-brown in summer, but changes to white in winter.

pg. 131 Anime Gamers - A chain of Japanese anime merchandise stores operated by BROCCOLI. The first US Gamers store opened in Los Angeles in 2001 (http://retail.animegamers.com).

pg. 131 Dejiko and Puchiko- Dejiko and Puchiko are mascots for Broccoli. Created by famed manga artist and author, Koge-Donbo, Dejiko and Puchiko have been featured in numerous manga, anime, and even videogames.

THINGS ARE GETTING A LITTLE WEIRD FOR THE ANGEL TROUPE.

MYSTERIOUS FORCES HAUNT THE ELLE CIEL, WREAKING HAVOC ON MINT'S FAVORITE DESSERT. WORSE STILL, THE ANGELS ARE SENT ON A MISSION TO THE PLANET OF NO RETURN, AND VANILLA HAS TO ADJUST TO THE RESPONSIBILITIES OF MOTHERHOOD. BUT NONE OF THIS CAN PREPARE THE ANGELS FOR THE STRANGEST THING OF ALL: FORTE HAS A DATE!

WHAT KIND OF PARTY IS THIS, ANYWAY!?

THE LIGHT TURNED ITSELF OFF.
MY CAKE MOVED ON ITS OWN.
AND MY STRAW-BERRY IS MISSING.
WHAT IS GOING ON!?
HUH!
COULD IT BE "THE THING?"
"THE THING" THAT GOES BOOGEDY BOOGEDY BOO!?
I MUST NOT PANIC.
BE COOL, MINT.
AN EYE FOR AN EYE...
...A TOOTH FOR A TOOTH.
Glare
NOW THEN...

TO FIGHT A GHOST...
...I MUST BECOME A GHOST!!
TIME FOR A COSTUME CHANGE!
...
FIRST, I SHOULD PROBABLY TURN ON THE LIGHT.
DARKNESS...
...IS DANGEROUS.
AH!
ゴツン THUD!
AAAHHH!
ガタン CLONK!
UGH!
AHH!
WHAT IS THAT SCREAMING?
NOOOOOO!!
パッ Flash

ギャラクシーエンジェル
Galaxy Angel β
BETA

WHEN CHITOSE JOINED THE IMPERIAL FORCES, SHE NEVER DREAMED THAT SHE'D END UP WORKING WITH HER IDOLS, THE ANGEL TROUPE. NOW THAT CHITOSE IS ON THE TEAM, THE ANGELS NEED HER TO JOIN THEM FOR A VERY SPECIAL MISSION: A GALAXY ANGEL VACATION!

AS MILFEULLE AND THE GANG GET ACQUAINTED WITH THEIR NEW TEAMMATE, THE ELLE CIEL IS FITTED WITH A NEW WEAPON FROM THE WHITE MOON. WHAT IS THIS STRANGE PIECE OF LOST TECHNOLOGY? CAN TAKUTO FIGURE OUT HOW TO USE IT? WITH MILFIE'S LUCK, THEY'D BETTER FIGURE IT OUT SOON!

THE NEW GALAXY ANGEL SERIES IS COMING SOON...

TO A STORE NEAR YOU!

IF WE'RE WITH TAKUTO...
...WE'LL BE ALRIGHT.
OUR VACATION IS OVER.
IT'S TIME TO START PLANNING.

UP TO NOW...
RIGHT AWAY,
...AND FROM NOW ON TOO.
COMMANDER TAKUTO!
Wow.
I HAVEN'T BEEN CALLED "COMMANDER" IN A WHILE.
Kinda tickles
WE FORGET YOUR TITLE, HUH?
Hahaha. Just Takuto!
Hey,
LET'S GET STARTED!
I want to get to the gym!

GALLERY

All you aspiring artists out there, now's your chance to show off your abilities. Broccoli Books might showcase your art in the upcoming volumes of Galaxy Angel Party.

Just send us your drawings or sketches featuring the Angel Troupe and their friends and you may be lucky enough to have your masterpiece appear in Galaxy Angel Party.

(Please, nothing pervy!)

Since images in the book will appear in black and white, there is a chance that color images will not appear in all their glory. But don't despair! For those drawings where black and white won't do them justice, we'll post your images in our Broccoli Books Blog! Just make sure to check out the Broccoli Books website following the publication of Galaxy Angel Party Volume 2.

For those of you who would like your Galaxy Angel artwork to be featured in Volume 2 or Volume 3 of Galaxy Angel Party, please send your drawing or sketch to:

Broccoli Books
Galaxy Angel Fan Art
P.O. Box 66078
Los Angeles, CA 90066

Don't forget to include your name and age!

NOW ONTO THE VOLUME 1 GALLERY!

Milfeulle
by Alex Gladbach, Age 13
San Antonio, TX

Mint on Vespa
by Fiona Vogel, Age 15
Houston, TX

Milfeulle
by Alex Gladbach, Age 13
San Antonio, TX

Milfeulle
by Barrie Thomas, Age 17
Menifee, CA

Ranpha
by Michelle Ho
Providence, RI

Takuto, Lester, Shatoyan "Soldiers for the Goddess"
by Barrie Thomas, Age 17
Menifee, CA

Mint
by Erin Simon, Age 10
Lynbrook, NY

Angel Troupe
by Sara Tanaka, Age 17
Honolulu, HI

Milfeulle
by Esteban "Ballanation" Paulos, Age 21
Albuquerque, NM

GA Animals
by Isidro Cristobal, Age 16
North Hollywood, CA

I Luv Mint
by Larry Goto, Age 13
Buffalo, NY

Ranpha
by Alison Kayes, Age 11
Reston, VA

Octopus Mint
by Rose Glover, Age 14
Baton Rouge, LA

OBEY Normad and Vanilla
by David Brasilia, Age 24
Baltimore, MD

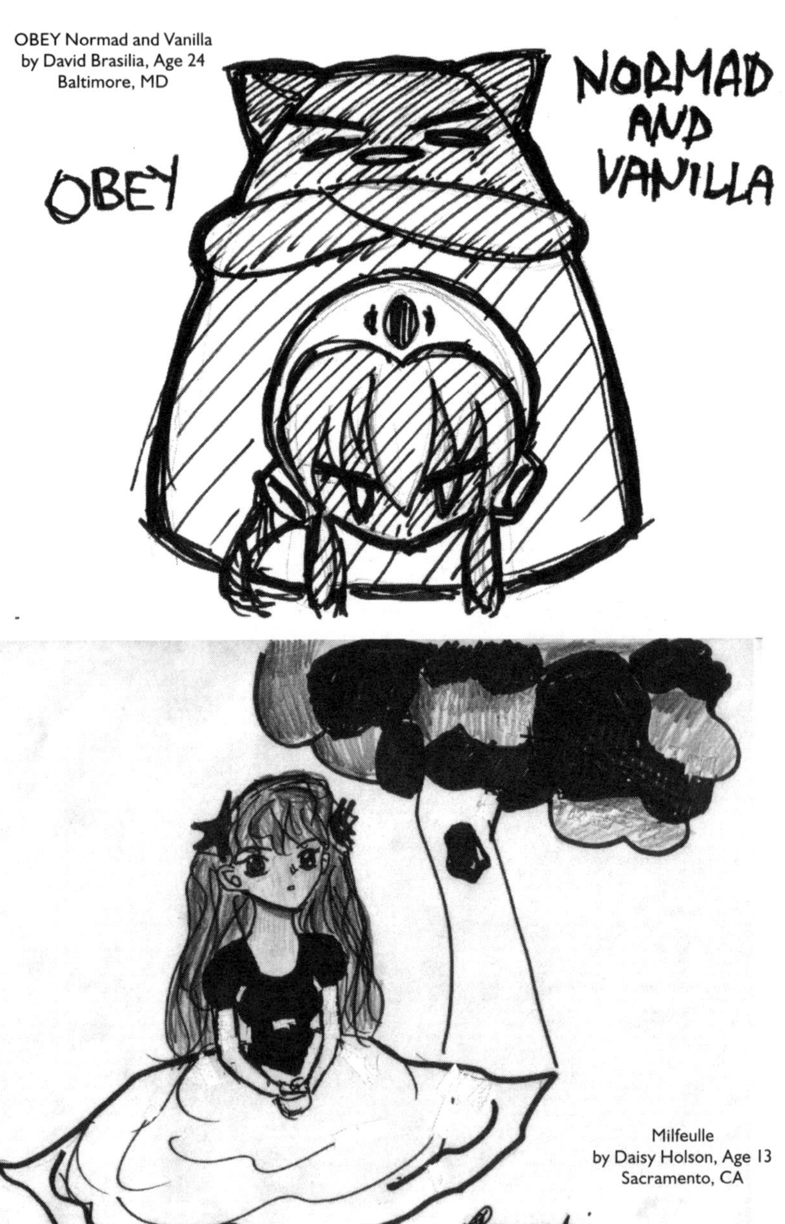

Milfeulle
by Daisy Holson, Age 13
Sacramento, CA

Haruhara Milfeulle
by Henry Chiu, Age 28
Chicago, IL

Galaxy Angels
by Shibata, Age 22
Los Angeles, CA

Galaxy Angel Spaceship
by Timothy O'Hare, Age 10
Boston, MA

Ranpha
by Ken Tay, Age 19
Burbank, CA

keychains

stickers

Mint cosplay trading plush

trading pins

postcards

trading figures

6" Mint statuette

Available at your local anime store

For more information visit:
www.bro-usa.com

ギャラクシーエンジェル
Galaxy Angel™ Merchandise

7" Milfeulle statuette

cell phone straps

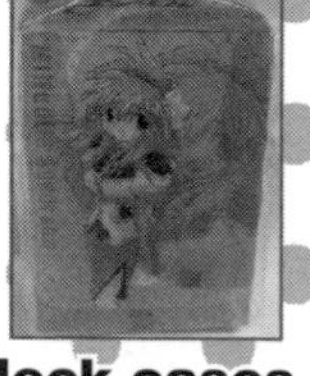

deck cases

mousepads

pencil boards

clear posters

clear stickers

Galaxy Angel™
by Kanan
NOT EVEN HEAVEN CAN HELP THESE ANGELS NOW.
Available now!
www.galaxyangel.net
BROCCOLI BOOKS™
www.bro-usa.com
© 2001, 2004 BROCCOLI
© 2001, 2004 Kanan. All Rights Reserved. First published in Japan by KADOKAWA SHOTEN PUBLISHING CO., LTD., Tokyo.

Try a bit of everything on the menu.

Galaxy Angel Z v.1 and 2
Stranded without Dessert

BANDAI
entertainment
www.bandai-ent.com

AVAILABLE NOW!

www.galaxyangel.net

A NEW TITLE COMING THIS SUMMER!
HE MUST RESTORE THE BALANCE OF THE SPIRITS KNOWN AS
KAMUI
AMID THE CHAOS,
THERE IS HOPE.
BROCCOLI BOOKS
www.bro-usa.com
© 2005 Shingo Nanami / SQUARE ENIX

Get Ready for Adventure!
ONLY DEJIKO AND HER FRIENDS
CAN SAVE THE GAMERS STORE!
DI GI CHARAT
THEATER
Dejiko's Adventure
TM
by Yuki Kiriga
brought to you by
BROCCOLI BOOKS
www.bro-usa.com

Di Gi Charat Theater™

Leave it to Piyoko!™

PLANET ANALOGUE WILL BE RICH!!

Join the celebration!
Di Gi Charat Theater - Leave it to Piyoko!, starring none other than Pyocola-sama, is out!

Support us, the Black Gema Gema Gang, and our mission to save Planet Analogue by buying the manga!!

Volume 2 coming soon to your local bookstores!

Di Gi Charat™
AVAILABLE IN MANGA AND DVD!
www.bro-usa.com
Di Gi Charat original TV series
Di Gi Charat the movie
Leave it to Piyoko!
*cover images subject to change.
Piyoko is Number One!
Piyoko is Number One!
Dejiko's Summer Vacation
Dejiko's Summer Vacation
Leave it to Piyoko!
Dejiko's Adventure
Di Gi Charat © 2005 BROCCOLI Illust. by Koge-Donbo
Di Gi Charat the Movie © 2001 BROCCOLI/Project Di Gi Charat THE Movie

STOP!
YOU'RE READING THE WRONG WAY!

This is the end of the book! In Japan, manga is generally read from right to left. All reading starts on the upper right corner, and ends on the lower left. American comics are generally read from left to right, starting on the upper left of each page. In order to preserve the true nature of the work, we printed this book in a right to left fashion. Those who are unfamiliar with manga may find this confusing at first, but once you start getting into the story, you will wonder how you ever read manga any other way!

THIS QUESTIONNAIRE IS REDEEMABLE FOR:

Galaxy Angel Playing Cards

Broccoli Books Questionnaire

Fill out and return to Broccoli Books to receive a deck of Galaxy Angel Playing Cards!*

PLEASE MAIL THE COMPLETE FORM, ALONG WITH UNUSED UNITED STATES POSTAGE STAMPS WORTH $4.00 ENCLOSED IN THE ENVELOPE TO:**

Broccoli International
Attn: Broccoli Books GA Cards Offer
P.O. Box 66078
Los Angeles, CA 90066

(Please write legibly)

Name: ______________________________

Address: ______________________________

City, State, Zip: ______________________________

E-mail: ______________________________

Gender: ☐ Male ☐ Female **Age:** _______

(If you are under 13 years old, parental consent is required)

Parent/Guardian signature: ______________________________

Occupation: ______________________________

Where did you hear about this title?

☐ Magazine (Please specify): ______________________________

☐ Flyer from: a store convention club other: ______________________________

☐ Website (Please specify): ______________________________

☐ At a store (Please specify): ______________________________

☐ Word of Mouth

☐ Other (Please specify): ______________________________

Where was this title purchased? (If known)

____

Why did you buy this title?

____

____

____

CUT ALONG HERE

How would you rate the following features of this manga?

	Excellent	Good	Satisfactory	Poor
Translation	☐	☐	☐	☐
Art quality	☐	☐	☐	☐
Cover	☐	☐	☐	☐
Extra/Bonus Material	☐	☐	☐	☐

What would you like to see improved in Broccoli Books manga?

____

Would you recommend this manga to someone else? ☐ Yes ☐ No

What related products would you be interested in?

☐ Posters ☐ Apparel Other: ______________________________

Which magazines do you read on a regular basis?

____

What manga titles would you like to see in English?

____

Favorite manga titles: ______________________________

Favorite manga artists: ______________________________

CUT ALONG HERE

What race/ethnicity do you consider yourself? (Please check one)

☐ Asian/Pacific Islander ☐ Native American/Alaskan Native
☐ Black/African American ☐ White/Caucasian
☐ Hispanic/Latino ☐ Other: ______________________________

Final comments about this manga:

____

____

____

Thank you!

* While supplies last.
** For residents of Canada, please send an International Reply Coupon (IRC) of $5.00 US made out to "Broccoli International."

All information provided will be used for internal purposes only. We will not sell or otherwise divulge any of the information.

Requests not in compliance with all terms of this form will not be acknowledged or returned. All submissions are subject to verification and become the property of Broccoli International USA. Fraudulent submission, including use of multiple addresses or P.O. boxes to obtain additional Broccoli International USA information or offers may result in prosecution. Broccoli International USA reserves the right to withdraw or modify any terms of this form. Void where prohibited, taxed, or restricted by law. Broccoli International USA will not be liable for lost, misdirected, mutilated, illegible, incomplete, or postage-due mail. This offer is only available to residents of the United States and Canada. For updates to the rules and regulations, please see www.bro-usa.com.